Praise for *His Cross and Ours*

"Seeing H. D. fulfilling a lifelong dream of writing a book has been the privilege of a lifetime. Its timeless message demonstrates what it looks like to be a true 'cross disciple' of Christ and provides readers with a guide who has seventy-five years of experience living that out. H. D. challenges us to thoughtfully and sincerely take up the cross and follow Jesus. As a twelve-year-old, I started attending University Baptist Church, and it was life changing. H. D. has significantly impacted my life, and I am truly grateful to still call him Pastor after fifty years of friendship!"

—JAMES BARNETT,
former president of DaySpring Cards, author of *Blue Skies*

"Insightful illumination of profound 'Z-life' wisdom! These truths are made clear and understandable. Thanks again, Pastor! I love this book as much as I imagined I would having known it needed to be written for the past forty-five years we've known each other! I thank God for you!"

—JIM BENTON,
Ventures for Christ board member

"My wife, Becky, and I sat under the teaching of Pastor McCarty for thirty-three years. It was an amazing experience to hear the Gospel come to life. H. D. again brings biblical truth to life for us in this book as he teaches us the significance of the cross. His ability to make the complex understandable is more than amazing. To God be the glory; great things he has done."

—SCOTT BULL,
former quarterback for the Arkansas Razorbacks
and the San Francisco 49ers, former CEO of Pace Industries Inc.

"Meeting H. D. McCarty over fifty years ago radically altered my life. H. D. has been my pastor, my boss, my father in the ministry, as well as my mentor and friend. *His Cross and Ours* contains the mature reflections of a seasoned spiritual warrior. With his lifetime of passionately pursuing Christ, Pastor McCarty points the way for sincere Christ-followers to fully embrace the cross. This book beckons the believer down the less-traveled path to liberating cross discipleship. I heartily endorse both author and book. Read it thoughtfully."

—Dr. Robert V. Cupp,
founding pastor of Fellowship Bible Church of Northwest Arkansas

"H. D. is an energetic warrior for the kingdom of God. He has always told me to 'stay in the battle.'"

—James E. Lindsey,
co-founder of Ventures for Christ,
chairman emeritus of Lindsey Management Co., Inc.

"Few people have had such a powerful, spiritual impact on so many as H. D. McCarty. I am one of those people H. D. has impacted. H. D. personally taught me to be a 'cross disciple.' For this, I will be forever grateful! But I'm even more thankful that now H. D.'s life-changing message is in writing. *His Cross and Ours* will challenge and, yes, change your life. I highly recommend it."

—Dr. Robert Lewis,
pastor, author, founder of BetterMan and Men's Fraternity

"H. D. McCarty is one of the finest men I know. I'm so thankful that he took the time to meet a freshman in the parking lot of Razorback Stadium in 1976. H. D. started our first conversation with this introduction: 'Hello, Houston! I am H. D. McCarty—I understand you have the same initials as I do! All great men are called by their initials. That's why you are called by your name, Houston, and not H. D.!

"H. D. played a tremendous role in my life. I went to listen to him every Sunday at University Baptist Church. He also came over to campus each week for a Razorback Bible study. H. D. was always so kind and so very wise. In 1998, Diana and I got our dream job and moved with our four children to the University of Arkansas in Fayetteville where I was to be head coach for the Razorback football team. Our family went to University Baptist Church because of H. D. McCarty! Our youngest, Haven, was baptized by H. D. I would also have H. D. speak to our Razorback teams to give our players a word of encouragement.

"It's very easy for me to say I endorse this wonderful book, because I know that each reader will gain insight that will help them in many ways with their life, especially with their personal relationship with God!"

—HOUSTON NUTT,
former University of Arkansas Razorback head coach (1998–2007),
former head coach at Murray State University and
Boise State University, three-time SEC Coach of the Year

"Ever since he recruited me to be an air force chaplain more than forty years ago, H. D. McCarty has been my faithful friend and selfless mentor. I'm immensely grateful for his wisdom and that these lessons on cross discipleship that he has lived before me and graciously shared with me in numerous conversations are now available to each new generation of Christ-followers. While H. D.'s life story will inspire you, the profound truth he shares in *His Cross and Ours* has the power to transform your life. Read it and you'll be encouraged to stay in the battle! Those who hunger to live the Christ-life more fully would do well to read the book once a year to reset their focus on the Savior and the cross he endured for our salvation."

—BOB PAGE,
US Air Force brigadier general and chief of chaplains (retired)

"His character, integrity, and personal passion for our Savior make endorsing this long-awaited book by our collegiate pastor, H. D. McCarty, an easy assignment. As were his sermons, so this book is all about the Lord Jesus and how we as 'cross disciples' are privileged to follow his example. This volume is a rich read, taking us to the Master, guiding us to his voice, and encouraging us to endure in our own cross walk as he did until we see our Savior face to face. Can't wait to read the real book with a pencil in hand and a prayer of gratitude for this man who taught me so much about Jesus the Christ."

—BARBARA RAINEY,
disciple of H. D., author, artist,
mom of six and mimi to twenty-seven,
co-founder of Family Life Today

"Finally, after more than seventy years . . . the book that H. D. has talked about writing, about the Son of Man he has walked with and the cross he has preached about . . . is *done*! I've been looking forward to this lifetime's work on the greatest Person who has ever lived and the greatest act of love that has ever been given, securing the greatest victory that has ever been won. As you read H. D.'s words about the death, burial, and resurrection of Jesus of Nazareth, you will find yourself drawing near to Jesus and see your life change because of his love and forgiveness."

—DENNIS RAINEY,
former collegiate pastor of University Baptist Church,
founder and former CEO and president of Family Life Today

"What you have in your hands is no ordinary book. It is a treasure trove of biblical principles and personal insights from the mind and heart of an apostolic leader who has walked with God for seventy-five years, impacting tens of thousands of lives in the process—including mine! Pastor H. D. McCarty has lifted and exalted Jesus more than any man I know. This book is his life and legacy to us all. So, read thoroughly, think deeply, and live differently!"

—STEVE SHADRACH,
founder of Student Mobilization, global ambassador for Via

"What can I say that can adequately describe this book and its author—affectionately known to us in the military as 'the squatty-bodied Rabbi'? Not much, for the title sums up the book's contents and H. D.'s life. From him I've learned the true progression of things: 'The Christ, the cross, the cost, and the crown.' Thank you, H. D., for leading us to the foot of the cross in surrender to Christ."

—TOM SMITH,
US Air Force colonel (retired),
command chaplain of the Arkansas National Guard

"The power of the cross and our response to that act of love is captured so clearly in Pastor McCarty's book."

—KEN STUCKEY,
Ventures for Christ board member

His Cross *and* Ours

HIS CROSS AND OURS

An Inspiring Call to Cross Discipleship

H. D. McCarty

HIS CROSS AND OURS
An Inspiring Call to Cross Discipleship

Copyright © 2024 by Ventures for Christ Inc.

Interior Layout and Design by Stephanie Anderson
Book Cover Design by Abigael Elliott

ISBN:
979-8-89165-113-5 *Paperback*
979-8-89165-114-2 *Hardback*
979-8-89165-115-9 *E-book*

Published by:
Streamline Books
Kansas City, MO
streamlinebookspublishing.com

STREAMLINE BOOKS

To Shirley
My wife, my mentor, my helper

In Memory of *J. Sidlow Baxter*

IN 1983 DURING HIS EIGHTIETH YEAR on this earth, I remember well my greatest mentor, J. Sidlow Baxter, preaching a sermon on Psalm 103 entitled "On Becoming an Octogenarian." Ever since, I have linked his wonderful friendship with me to this magnificent psalm. Now that Shirley and I have experienced our eighties, I feel as if we finally understand the full meaning of his message!

Sidlow was the constant spiritual father I never had. For twenty-five wonderful years, he was a guiding presence in both my life and the spiritual life of University Baptist Church in Fayetteville, Arkansas, through his preaching visits. He spoke at University Baptist Church more than any other guest pastor we ever had! Sidlow graduated from Charles Spurgeon's Metropolitan Tabernacle Seminary in London in 1928. He pastored three churches in England, leading them each to greatness, and even turned down Metropolitan's invitation to be their pastor in 1938 (at the time, it was the most famous church in England). After World War II, Sidlow began his international ministry of biblical teaching and writing. He authored more than thirty books, two of which—*Explore the Book* and *Awake My Heart*—were translated into several different languages and sold more than a million copies each (and that was before the internet and Amazon). As I write this, I'm once again using Sidlow's *Awake My Heart* in the mornings during my quiet time. His insight and theological grasp are always amazing and centered on our Savior.

Throughout our close friendship, Sidlow always referred to me as Harvey, calling it "a good English name." I can distinctly remember one phone call when an eighty-seven-year-old Sidlow inquired, "Tell me, Harvey, what *is* email?" I tried to explain it to him as best I could. When I finished, there was silence on the line. When he finally spoke up, he said, "I am so out of touch with all this modernity, but I suppose as long as I am in touch with him, I'll have no worries!" Another time, Sidlow proclaimed regarding his golden years: "Old age is wonderful. I wouldn't have missed it for the world! If it were not for these plumbing problems with the old body, it would be heaven on earth!"

Of the many Spirit-taught comments I could make about aging when remembering Sidlow, I'll limit myself to two. First, old age is God's idea, and we know that the Lord doesn't have any bad ideas! Second, I have learned that you must actually practice getting older before you begin to discover how young you really are spiritually. What a blessed experience! As Sidlow's sermon made clear, growing old is the only way you can fully encounter the transformative power of Psalm 103 in your life and experience "your youth" truly being "renewed like the eagles" (Ps. 103:5).

In January 2000, I was asked by his widow, Isa, to speak at Sidlow's funeral in Santa Barbara, California. I felt it was the perfect picture of a mouse being asked to honor an elephant. It is my hope that this serves to further celebrate such a wise mentor, dedicated pastor, prolific author, dear friend, and spiritual father in Christ.

Dedication

FOR OVER SIXTY-SIX YEARS, my greatest, most undeserved treasure next to knowing the Lord Jesus has been my precious wife, Shirley. When I first met her at Baylor University, I was a pilot in the United States Air Force stationed near Waco, Texas. I thought she was the most beautiful woman I had ever seen, and she remains that to this day! I was thrilled and greatly honored when she agreed to marry me in 1957. She thought she was marrying a man destined for a career in the air force, but she was totally supportive when I felt the Lord leading us into ministry.

With a graciousness, patience, and kindness that only the Holy Spirit can give, Shirley has been the epitome of a mate and mother. Throughout more than sixty-six years of church and discipleship ministry, she has been my helpmate in every way. I have never had to worry or be concerned with her response to times of testing, challenges, or difficult situations. Shirley directed the seventh grade Sunday school class and had many other teaching and training responsibilities throughout the years. She continually blessed our church family and me with her beautiful singing voice. Over the years, Shirley has been an exceptional mother who consistently prioritized her children, always involved with their needs and activities. She has splendidly transitioned into the roles of loving grandmother and great-grandmother—her favorite roles by far!

My sweet wife knows my struggles and failings yet steadfastly loves and prays for me always! The Lord has used her to bless my ministry in a way I never could have known without her. She has dedicated her life to loving and supporting me, being the spiritual center for our family as well as serving and ministering to countless others. It is truly to her that I am the most appreciative and indebted. Her strengths have protected our family, and I love her dearly.

I dedicate this book to her in honor of the Lord Jesus as we both continue to seek out his cross and all that the Lord has for us in these sunset years on earth!

Contents

Foreword

EVEN AS A HIGH SCHOOL student in the small town of Hope, Arkansas, I had heard of H. D. McCarty, the Pastor of University Baptist Church in Fayetteville and known as the "Chaplain of the Razorbacks." In my first semester at Ouachita Baptist University, I first heard Dr. McCarty in person as he came to speak to students on the campus. I still vividly remember his dynamic delivery of a message that was packed with biblical conviction, cultural clarity, and persuasive passion. Over the next fifty years of my life, I would come to personally know Dr. H. D. McCarty and would become an unapologetic follower of his ministry.

At a point of my life when some of my dreams and hopes collapsed in a pile of ashes and when almost no one called, it was H. D. McCarty who reached out to me and lifted me spiritually and financially out of the pit into which I had fallen after the difficult loss of an election. There was nothing in it for Dr. McCarty. He didn't need me for anything, but he sensed I needed him. His sensitivity to the Holy Spirit in reaching out to me was one of what would become repeated reminders of his willingness to forego his own interests to lift up a fellow believer who simply needed the encouragement to stay in the arena and answer the next bell.

When I was to be sworn in as governor, I insisted that H. D. McCarty be the keynote speaker at the prayer service prior to the inauguration. He became my trusted mentor and an always available confidante no matter the crisis.

When he told my wife, Janet, and me that he would pray for us every day, she replied, "How about twice a day?" And there was not a time after that in which my esteemed personal "Rabbi" failed to affirm that he had indeed prayed for us not once, but TWICE a day. There is NO one I'd rather have in my corner mentioning my name to God than H. D. McCarty.

Over these fifty years, I came to realize what a remarkable man H. D. McCarty is. The second-ever chaplain in the US Air Force to rise to the rank of brigadier general in the two-hundred-fifty-year history of the American militia, he is unsurpassed in his patriotism and devoted service to his country. As a biblical scholar, he amazes me with his capacity to glean the most profound applications of the principles of the Holy Writ in such a simple manner to bring home a point so that a young child or a tenured university professor could equally understand.

Everywhere I traveled, I met leaders in ministry, business, sports, and government whose lives were significantly impacted by the ministry of H. D. McCarty. It was a statement of truth that the sun never set on the ministry of Dr. McCarty because it was being lived out in churches, the mission field, the classroom, the halls of government, or the boardrooms of the most successful corporations on earth.

I've read bestselling books authored by those whose lives were touched by his ministry. Some of the largest Christian organizations on earth are led by those who once sat under his teaching. Some of the most influential pastors on the planet were discipled by H. D. McCarty.

Those of us who know and love him have urged him to write "his book." Not a topical book of contemporary themes, but a book about his journey, what he had learned, how he persevered through the tough times, and what has kept him fresh and filled with insights from his twenties to his nineties and still going. After all these years, he's finally completed the book that many of us have longed for, waited for, and now get to explore its pages. It took him a lifetime to write, because it took him a lifetime to live.

I've often said to people that if ANYONE ever said an unkind word about H. D. McCarty in my presence, they need to be prepared for a fight with a buzz saw! If H. D. McCarty asked me to crawl over broken glass, I wouldn't enjoy it, but I'd sure give it my best shot!

I love H. D. McCarty. And as you read this remarkable book, you will too.

MIKE HUCKABEE,
former governor of Arkansas

Preface

I was born on November 4, 1932. My father, Harvey Dwight Roseberry Topp, was a Canadian who had moved to San Antonio, Texas, for work, which was where he met my mother, Vera Whitley. After getting married, my parents were transferred to Oklahoma City, Oklahoma, where I was born. Shortly after my birth, we moved back to San Antonio. It was during this time that my father contracted a terminal blood disease that left him too weak to work. My aunt would later recall that whenever I would run over to him as a toddler and reach my hands up, he didn't even have the strength to lift me. While my father was ill, my mother worked five and a half days a week to support our family, including her teenage sister. However, during Labor Day weekend in 1935, my father committed suicide in our garage. He did so immediately after I told him it was time for dinner. He told me he'd be right in. But the next thing I remember is people filling our garage and my mother shaking him and calling out "Dwight . . . Dwight!" I even remember the bullet mark in his forehead. What agony must have been in my dying father's heart as he spoke his final words to me. It remains the only memory I have of him.

In January 1939, my mother married my stepfather, Jack McCarty, and shortly thereafter we moved to Dallas, Texas, where I would spend the rest of my childhood and my college years alongside my two half-siblings. Around this time, my mother began calling me by my initials instead of Harvey, since my full name reminded her of my father. From that point on, whenever I would introduce myself to people, I would refer to myself as H. D. (all great men go by their initials).

During the summer of 1946 when I was thirteen years old, I took a bus trip by myself from Dallas to Alberta, Canada, to visit family. The day after returning home to Texas, I woke up with a terrible headache. I remember my mother driving me to Parkland Hospital, where the doctors told her that I had both bulbar polio and spinal meningitis. At that time, I was not a Christian and had never once prayed for my healing, although I later learned from one of my aunts that my mother had asked people to come to our house to pray for me. After staying in the hospital for a month, I returned home where I gave myself penicillin shots. By that fall, I had recovered enough to attend school, and I never looked back.

I attended the Highland Park Independent School District in Dallas, where I started to become interested in music. Having no idea what instrument I wanted to play, I went to the band teacher, Mr. Taylor, who handed me a beat-up mellophone. From there, I took up the French horn and played the drums in a jazz band with some of my friends, playing gigs all over Dallas. And I was good (real good). It was those skills as a musician that would eventually earn me a band scholarship to Southern Methodist University in Dallas.

Besides developing a love for music in high school, I also became a Christian during this time. For months, a couple of my friends had been trying to get me to go to a home Bible study where some of my classmates were regulars. Although I had been attending church since I was eleven, I wasn't a Christian. I was a seventeen-year-old high school senior who had no interest in the Bible, much less a spiritual thought in my body. I was too busy practicing and traveling with my band to go to Bible study. Music was my god. I was going to be a famous jazz drummer—the next Gene Krupa! Finally, in March of 1950, I agreed to go. The Bible study was taught by a Dallas Theological Seminary student named Verd Holsteen. A veteran of World War II, Verd was in his mid-twenties at that time and was serving as an unpaid volunteer at the request of some church members who were concerned about their high school students.

After I had attended a couple of studies and asked him a lot of questions, Verd took an interest in me and even offered to come by my house to go through the curriculum he had planned for the entire year. On Saturday, March 28, 1950, Verd came over and, after talking for a while, asked me if I knew what a Christian was. I sincerely said it was someone who lives in America and helps old ladies. He then wanted to know if I had ever prayed before. I replied that the only time I could remember praying was before my high school exams! Finally, Verd asked me if I had ever asked Christ into my life, something no one had ever asked me before. I realized at that moment that my life was empty of God and that I was a sinner involved in some bad things. I felt a deep sense of guilt because I had ignored and offended Jesus. So Verd and I prayed together right there, and I asked the Lord to forgive me and come into my life to help me.

I'll never forget the moment we bowed our heads together and I asked the Savior to forgive me for all I had done and for who I was. I asked Jesus to be my Lord and to make me who I should be! It was there that I sensed something new, something I had never felt before. For the first time, I sensed that I was cleansed of my sin. I didn't feel guilty, and I wanted to be closer to the Lord. For the next two years, Verd and I met weekly as he discipled me to know and love the Savior, study Scripture, and constantly listen to the Spirit. My new mind and heart eagerly anticipated those weekly meetings. Those times with Verd laid the foundation for all I am today.

When I think back now to what happened to me way back on March 28, 1950, the moment that Christ came into my life, I remain continually overwhelmed by inexpressible thanksgiving. On that day, my mind, life purpose, destiny, desires, vision, and being were instantly transformed by the Creator of heaven and earth. The God of the cosmos touched my little life, and I recognized it! He sent Verd into my life to make plain to me my deepest need to ask God's Son, Jesus Christ, into my life as my Savior and Lord. I remain continually overwhelmed in eternal gratitude for that. Can you imagine the coordination that the Lord was working there? Verd not only led me to Christ but also gave me the discipleship foundation that would last a lifetime. I have tried to follow his example ever since.

After graduating high school, I attended Southern Methodist University (SMU), where I earned my bachelor's degree in 1955. While attending SMU, I signed up for the US Air Force ROTC and was commissioned as a second lieutenant into active duty upon graduation, thus following my boyhood dream to become an air force pilot. I entered flight school that summer and was awarded my pilot wings in August of 1956 at Vance Air Force Base in Enid, Oklahoma. I was then transferred to James Connally Air Force Base in Waco, Texas, to earn my navigator and bombardier wings and become triple-rated (meaning I was trained as a pilot, navigator, and bombardier).

One weekend shortly after I moved back to Texas, I went to the SMU vs Baylor University football game. After the game, a number of us were invited to the house of one of my old high school friends. It was there that I met Shirley Ann DeBerry. Shirley was a high school homecoming queen and was named a "Baylor Beauty" both years she attended the university. I got Shirley's number later from the same friend, and (surprise) we were married in 1957, only ten months after our first date.

During the first year of our marriage, I was stationed at Little Rock Air Force Base, where I flew B-47 and RB-47 aircraft, before moving again to Chennault Air Force Base in Lake Charles, Louisiana. It was in Lake Charles in 1959 that our daughter, Karen, was born. During this time, I was sent on assignment to England in the midst of the Cold War. As a triple-rated pilot, I was assigned to fly a six-engine bomber loaded with an atomic bomb. If the Soviets attacked, our mission would have been to fly into Russia and drop the bomb forty miles south of Moscow. We were never called into action, and this would be the closest I ever came to facing actual combat. Over my entire active-duty career in the air force, I logged more than fifteen hundred hours of flight time while piloting a number of different aircraft.

In September of 1959, I was released from the air force. It was during my time on active duty that I first started to feel the call to Christian ministry. In 1960, I started attending Southwestern Baptist Theological Seminary in Fort Worth, Texas, where I earned my Master of Divinity degree in 1964. While attending seminary, our son, Kevin, was born in 1961. Also, I joined the Air Force Reserves 69th Troop Carrier Squadron out of Carswell Air Force Base near Fort Worth, where I flew C-119 aircraft. I later left flying status and became the commander of the Headquarters Squadron Section until I was asked to serve the unit as their chaplain in November of 1963. In doing so, I am one of the few individuals in the air force who can say they served the same unit as a pilot, a squadron commander, and a chaplain!

Believe it or not, when I was in seminary, the last thing that I wanted to do was be a Baptist pastor! I had three goals for myself upon graduating from seminary. First, I wanted to stay in the air force, place my cross on top of my wings, and continue my chaplaincy work. Second, I wanted to practice ministry that specifically influenced students (during seminary I served as a Young Life leader at the university and worked as a youth pastor). And third, I wanted to get my doctorate from Southwestern. (I have to confess that I selfishly thought "Dr. McCarty" had a nice ring to it.) However, during one of my graduate seminars, my professor Dr. John Newport announced that the pastor of University Baptist Church in Fayetteville, Arkansas, had recently left and they were looking for someone to fill the position. I had little interest in moving to Arkansas. I rebelled against the idea of being just another preacher. Despite all this, I wanted to be where the Lord wanted me and felt torn about what I should do. I had been attending a

Presbyterian church before marrying my wife, Shirley, who had been raised in the Baptist church. In trying to determine which denomination I should be a part of, my Presbyterian pastor told me: "H, you're a Jesus man. You will be able to serve him wherever he leads you!" I ended up walking over to Dr. Newport's office and turning in my résumé for the position in Arkansas, with no expectation whatsoever that I'd be selected.

Evidently, the folks at University Baptist Church saw some potential in me because they invited me to interview for the role. All that being said, I was still pretty torn over whether I should serve as an air force chaplain, take a position in student ministry, stay in Fort Worth and work on my doctorate at Southwestern, or move to Arkansas. While I was struggling with my fourfold decision, I had an unplanned discussion with the education director of the church I was working at in Fort Worth. He was a godly man and a good friend who knew all about my situation. He asked me if I knew what I was going to do about University Baptist Church. I told him I wasn't sure what the Lord's will was and that I hadn't made up my mind yet.

He responded, "Well, H, are you willing to do any of those four things for the Lord?"

I said that yes, I was.

He replied, "H, you can't make a mistake if you're ready to do any one of those things that the Lord might want."

Man, that brought liberty to my heart. What a godsend it was for me to recognize the brilliance and power of those words! Since then, I've reflected on that moment a couple hundred times (or more) in my life. Would you do *any of these things* for the Lord? Yes, if the Lord tells me to do it! It dawned on me then and there that I should at least visit the church so that I could be properly informed before making my decision. I made the long drive from Fort Worth to Fayetteville and arrived at University Baptist Church. After touring the building and talking to the lovely people, I felt an inviting warmth about the place. Soon after, I was offered the job and, at the age of thirty-two, I became the senior pastor of University Baptist Church. (I still don't know why they picked me.) It was to be the first and *only* church I would ever pastor!

While serving at University Baptist, my dream of reaching students began to come to overwhelming fruition. When I arrived at the church in 1965, we had fewer than two hundred people attending our Sunday service and fewer than twenty-five students; we even had to rope off the back rows of pews to push people toward the front to make the sanctuary feel less empty! But over time we began to attract more and more students from the University of Arkansas. Our services steadily grew over the next several years, and before long, we were hosting three services every Sunday, drawing a couple thousand people across the entire day. At one point, almost a fourth of the entire undergraduate population was attending University Baptist Church!

During my entire thirty-nine-year career at the church, we ministered to approximately twenty thousand university students. Isn't that something! We eventually expanded from our four-hundred-and-fifty-person auditorium to a new thirteen-hundred-seat sanctuary, which equipped us to start a number of new ministries that reached out to our community. By the time I retired in 2004, University Baptist Church had grown into one of the largest churches in the state of Arkansas.

Throughout my time as the senior pastor at University Baptist Church, I was involved in several other ministry opportunities as well. The Lord blessed me with the opportunity to continue my role as an air force reserve chaplain in Arkansas in 1965. In May of 1976, I was assigned as a chaplain for the 188th Combat Support Squadron of the Air National Guard, and starting in December of 1983, I began serving as the chaplain for the entire Arkansas Air National Guard. I was appointed to the Air National Guard Chaplain Advisory Group in July 1984, and on July 16, 1986, I was selected as an assistant to the air force chief of chaplains and promoted to the rank of brigadier general. As a result, I can humbly boast that I am the only triple-rated chaplain general in the history of the air force! During my time in the military, I had the privilege of ministering to hundreds of service members ranging from high-ranking Pentagon officials to newly enlisted personnel in the hangers.

My efforts to minister to the community of Fayetteville extended beyond the church sanctuary. I served on the regional board of governors for our hospital and was the first clergy member to serve on the local chamber of commerce. For almost thirty years, I served as the chaplain of the University of Arkansas Razorbacks. The players even dubbed me the "Razorback Rabbi."

During this time, I also had a television ministry program that ran weekly across the state, and I established and taught at the Arkansas Institute of Theology, a biblical education program that ministered to more than fifteen hundred people during its twenty-five-year run. While serving at University Baptist Church, I also achieved my dream of becoming "Dr. McCarty" by doing doctoral studies at several institutions, culminating in earning my PhD from the California Graduate School of Theology in 1983. Upon earning my doctorate, I served as an adjunct professor at several academic institutions, including John Brown University, Southern Baptist Theological Seminary, and my alma mater, Southwestern Baptist Theological Seminary.

In 2004, after thirty-nine years at University Baptist Church, I felt the call to step away from full-time professional ministry and retire from my position as senior pastor. My thirty-nine years of ministry at University Baptist Church fulfilled the words of our Lord's promise to me in Psalm 37:4: "Take delight in the Lord, and he will give you the desires of your heart." Before I moved to Arkansas, I envisioned spending my life serving in the air force, working with college students, getting my doctorate, and teaching. I never pictured becoming a Baptist pastor! But being willing to trust God and, above all, delight in him first rather than pursuing my own desires not only gave me the true delight of my heart— serving as a pastor—but also added the bonuses of what I *thought* I desired most—air force chaplaincy, student ministry, and earning my doctorate. The Lord fulfilled all three of my initial desires through the one desire I didn't have or want! How about that? I praise him for this great lesson!

The year I retired from University Baptist Church, I had the honor of opening the United States Senate in prayer during the National Day of Prayer. I also spoke at the Normandy American Cemetery in France while commemorating the sixtieth anniversary of D-Day. As I entered a new season of my ministry career, I established Ventures for Christ ministries, feeling a call to continue the work of teaching, inspiring, writing, and discipling people for Jesus's sake. Since my retirement, Ventures for Christ has been a wonderful tool through which I have been able to continue sharing my love for our Messiah and proclaiming his glory to the world.

As I enter the ninety-first year of my life on earth and my seventy-fourth year as a Christian, I find myself increasingly consumed with the youthful spirit of Caleb who, at the ripe age of eighty-five, proclaimed to Joshua that he was "still as strong today as the day Moses sent me out; I'm just as vigorous to go out to battle now as I was then" (Josh. 14:11). Like Caleb (and at his age!) I am still seeking opportunities during my last years to conquer the remaining mountains the Lord has set before me! I want to keep growing so that I can continue to share with everyone the liberating richness of discovering, enduring, and carrying our cross just as our Savior carried his. At the same time, I feel that Paul's words about having "fought the good fight"—in Greek, literally "agonized the good agony" (*ton kalon agōna* ēgōnismai)—and "finished the race" are finally becoming my own as I sense my own departure coming closer (2 Tim. 4:7). I want to fulfill the ministry path that I still see set before me by the Master. As my time on earth runs out, I yearn for the time I have left to be the most fruitful, effective, and blessed by him as possible. I have no fear, only a relaxed urgency to fully please our dear Savior while I can!

My hope is that my story and this book—the culmination of a long life of public ministry, personal struggle, theological reflection, and increased "yieldedness" to our Lord Jesus—may inspire, instruct, and guide you on your own journey of cross discipleship.

Joyfully stay in the battle, my brothers and sisters in Christ.

H. D. McCarty
In my seventy-fifth year of serving the Lord
Fayetteville, Arkansas
April 2024

"I have spoken to you with great frankness;
I take great pride in you.
I am greatly encouraged;
in all our troubles my joy knows no bounds."

—2 CORINTHIANS 7:4

Introduction

ONE SURPRISING FACT ABOUT THE New Testament that I find absolutely fascinating is that the only time Jesus explicitly mentions the "cross" (*stauros* in Greek) is in the context of one single command: "Whoever wants to be my disciple must deny themselves and take up their cross daily and follow me" (Luke 9:23b). While Jesus repeats this decree five times throughout Matthew, Mark, and Luke, he doesn't explicitly reference the cross again in the Gospels. Elsewhere, Jesus talks about his crucifixion and his death, but never his cross. How about that?

The cross is one of the deepest and most important topics in the study of theology, if not *the* most important. After all, the salvific message of the Savior's cross doesn't just matter for Baptists or Methodists, for fundamentalists or charismatics, for Protestants or Catholic Christians—it matters for *all humanity* and uniquely so for those who claim Jesus as their Savior. Indeed, the words from the lips of Jesus in Luke 9:23 extend out to *all people* who seek to follow the Messiah. But what does this message really mean? What does "taking up" one's cross actually look like? How might acting upon Jesus's command in Luke 9:23 practically change how you and I live our daily lives?

As its title suggests, this book explores the relationship between Jesus's cross and the cross he commands us to take up as we follow him. It is the product of a lifetime of theological research and ministry experience. In the following chapters, we'll examine together the historical events surrounding Jesus's crucifixion; the lessons his sacrificial death teaches us; and the ways in which his cross models how we, as Christians, should obey his order to take up, carry, endure, understand, and hang upon our own personal crosses. Before moving forward in our discussion, however, it would be helpful to first explain what I mean when talking about being a "cross disciple."

DEFINITION OF CROSS DISCIPLESHIP

One of the Scripture passages children often memorize in Sunday school is John 3:16: "For God so loved the world that he gave his one and only Son, that whoever believes in him shall not perish but have eternal life." Its meaning has kept expanding for me throughout my life as my understanding of his truth has grown! In many ways, we might read John 3:16 as the basis for a definition of what it means to be a cross disciple. From John 3:16, we learn what the *purpose, power,* and *promise* of the cross are all about both for Jesus and for us as we are called to imitate his life.

The first part of John 3:16 reveals the *purpose of cross discipleship*: love. As we will see in chapter 1, Jesus died the most agonizing death known to humanity upon the cross out of his *love* for the entire world. In the words of Paul, "God demonstrates his own love for us in this: While we were still sinners, Christ died for us" (Rom. 5:8). Just as Christ died on *his cross* out of love for humanity, so too those of us who decide to take up *our cross* must be motivated by the same sacrificial love. This is exactly what Jesus himself declares in the Gospel of John: "A new command I give you: Love one another. As I have loved you, so you must love one another" (John 13:34).

The second part of John 3:16 reveals the salvific *power behind cross discipleship*. Out of his perfect love for the world, the Father "gave his one and only Son" on humanity's behalf. Elsewhere in Scripture, we learn more fully what this means. Jesus came "to seek and to save the lost" (Luke 19:10) so that those "who believed in his name, he gave the right to become children of God" (John 1:12). In the words of Paul, our fallen world was saved through Jesus's sacrificial death and suffering, for "while we were God's enemies, we were reconciled to him through the death of his Son" (Rom. 5:10). As the book of Hebrews puts it, the power of the cross means that Jesus "is able to save completely those who come to God through him, because he always lives to intercede for them" (Heb. 7:25). Jesus is praying for you and me right now. Amazing!

However, it is critical to remember that the power of the cross does not stop at our salvation. Throughout this book, we'll discover that when Jesus died on the cross, he also sanctified us so that we, too, could "work out" our own salvation (Phil. 2:12). As cross disciples, we have been empowered by the sacrificial love of Messiah Jesus and the Holy Spirit (Rom. 5:5) so that we may live out our lives for God's glory (1 Cor. 10:31). Each and every one of us has a part to play in God's redemption story and his reconciliation of humanity!

Finally, the third part of John 3:16 reveals the *promise that follows* from the salvific power of the cross. By giving up his one and only Son to death upon the cross, God ensured that "whoever believes in him shall not perish but have eternal life." Through Jesus's death, God has promised us life everlasting—a new heaven and a new earth (Rev. 21). As Paul writes, through Jesus Christ we have been given the promise of a new heavenly citizenship, one that "will transform our lowly bodies so that they will be like his glorious body" (Phil. 3:20–21). I'll never forget my moment of reconciliation when I asked the Lord Jesus to save me and be my Lord. I was right with God for the first time in my life. I began a wonderful process of change, and I haven't stopped changing ever since.

The promise of life everlasting that comes from Jesus's cross is more than just a future reality. It also shapes our present response! Just as in *our death* we will join with Jesus in eternal life, so too in *our lives* we are called to follow his cross-carrying and cross-hanging example. We are to be like him in life *and* in death! As we will see in the following chapters, our most abundant life as cross disciples arises when we seek to fulfill the cross mission that God has recruited us for. We have been called to "bear much fruit" for God's glory, showing ourselves to be his disciples (John 15:8). This means taking up our own individual crosses, just as the Savior took up his.

We will talk in more detail about what this means in the pages to follow. For now, we can summarize being a cross disciple as acting out of sacrificial love through the salvific power of Jesus's cross while seeking to follow Christ's cross-carrying and cross-hanging example. To put it more simply, *being a cross disciple means doing something for someone else that is spiritually centered in Christ and his cross*. The greater the need, difficulty, or pressure that comes from helping someone else come to know Christ and grow closer to him, the more costly your cross is! This is not just an occasional thing; we are instructed to take up our cross *each and every day*!

UNDERSTANDING THE CROSS AND THE MESSIAH'S LOVE

Of course, in order to truly understand what it means for us to be cross disciples, we must constantly seek to better understand the deepest meaning of Jesus's cross. We cannot comprehend *our cross* unless we authentically encounter *his cross*! As Hebrews 5 points out, Jesus is the Father's perfect Son who became incarnate upon the earth. Yet, even as God's Son, he remained obedient to the Father through the immense and degrading suffering he experienced upon the cross. Christ came to earth knowing that this was the only way to perfectly solve the problem of our rebellion and brokenness. He knew he had to triumph over the suffering of his cross in order to fulfill the Father's will.

In many ways, I believe we need to think about our lives the way Jesus thought about his. Jesus knew that he wasn't going to get through his life on earth without going through the cross. And he *still* went through with it! Man, that's the way you and I ought to live! If you've genuinely decided to follow Jesus, you're going to have to suffer your cross too. You can't avoid it if you're truly following him. It is by carrying and hanging upon the crosses we have been called to bear that we encounter the authentic Jesus. And, just like Jesus, we will never master this life unless we conquer our crosses. *That is why I wrote this book*: to help others master their own cross-carrying missions!

I assure you, dear reader, just as Jesus showed during his own cross-centered life and crucifixion, none of this is easy. We need to understand that bearing our cross, becoming a servant of the living God, and loving others all take incredible—even sacrificial—endurance, as I'll explain in more detail in chapter 3. Every day, cross disciples across the world are attacked in various ways as they seek to follow the Father's will. After all, the authentic cross of Christ is an insult to the devil and is despised by the world! Indeed, bearing your cross can bring about agonizing suffering. This is why many Christians show up on Sundays but don't want to take any part of the cross the rest of the week. That's because the cross rips us from our own vain glory and delivers us into the presence of the Son of God. Whether we like it or not, *the real cross demands everything from us*. It means death to our very self.

When thinking about the demands of the cross, I can't help but think of a story I read recently. During air combat in the South Pacific in World War II, a young second lieutenant who was flying into battle for the first time became separated from his formation as four enemy fighters suddenly pounced on him. These aircraft were manned by experienced pilots who, unlike the young lieutenant, had flown many times before. The lieutenant knew he didn't have a chance against these enemy fighters and was desperately trying to get away from them, wondering what on earth he could possibly do at this point. He knew his death was imminent. But all of a sudden, he saw another aircraft approaching! Out of the blue, his squadron commander bounced into the fray, his voice coming in strong over the intercom: "I've got him." Almost immediately, the commander shot down two of the enemy aircraft and damaged the third. But while this was happening, the fourth enemy aircraft shot down the squadron commander, his aircraft crashing into the sea. Luckily for the young lieutenant, the fourth and final enemy airplane was out of ammunition, and it flew off. All the young lieutenant had to do was fly back to base. There was nothing else the enemy could do to him—*the threat had been eliminated.*

The inexperienced lieutenant was safe because of what his squadron commander did for him—because of the sacrifice he made. The commander took all the sting out of the enemy. And that's exactly what Christ did for us on the cross! The main difference, however, is that while the lieutenant could only report the sad news that his valiant squadron commander was dead, we can joyfully report that our Savior has conquered death and we will live with him forever! *Christ has taken the sting out of death and the evil of this sinful world.* He's there right in front of us to fight the battles that we cannot handle on our own, if only we recognize him, so that we may fly safely home. Believe me, that doesn't mean it'll be easy! There will always be storms and anxieties in life that we'll need to navigate through. Cross discipleship will always involve suffering, sacrifice, and struggle. But we can take comfort in knowing that the big battle—Christ's crucifixion on our behalf—has already been won for us. We're destined for heaven. *We're destined for home.*

As I hope to show in this book, being a cross disciple involves playing our small part in God's salvific plan for humanity. On his cross, Jesus bore the burden of sin and death, a burden that none of us could have ever bore on our own. (If we could have, then he would not have had to come and carry it himself!) While the cross we are called to bear is certainly different than his, we must still do so with the same purpose as our Savior. God sent his Son to the cross in order to redeem a dense, hopeless, confused, rebellious, and guilty humanity and bring us back to him. He did this not because we deserved it, but solely *because he loved us.*

The loving and sacrificial way that Jesus approached his cross models the attitudes and actions we should adopt when it comes to our own cross missions. For Jesus, his self-denial in leaving heaven, his incarnation, the repudiation of the mankind he came to save, the agony of crucifixion, and his own "separation" from the Father were all procedural to the purpose of his cross. *All of this he did out of love.* As cross disciples, we are both invited and commanded to join him in carrying a cross with the same purposeful and sacrificial love that he did as our Messiah. As Luke 9:23 states, this means denying ourselves and our wants and desires, taking up our cross mission as a priority, and accepting the circumstances and conditions required to bring his love to others as we attempt to follow him.

As you can tell, the love that took Jesus to his crucifixion—the same love we are called to incarnate as we accept our duty and privilege as cross disciples—is so much more than a casual, happy, or sentimental kindness. The Messiah's love is a robust, demanding, exacting, compelling, never-ending dedication that radically gives the object of that love the very best that God can offer. When we carry our cross just as Jesus did, we embrace the praise and obedience that pleases God. It is this kind of love that offers the riches of significance, power, strength, and righteousness in Christ Jesus our Lord to others. Only this kind of love manifests and demonstrates the abundant life promised to us by the Savior: "I have come that they may have life, and have it to the full" (John 10:10b).

CHAPTER SUMMARIES

The following investigation of Jesus's cross and our calling to cross discipleship is divided into six chapters.

Chapter 1 provides the foundation for this book by examining the historical evidence behind Jesus's arrest, trials, and crucifixion, including the testimony of the New Testament Gospels and the supplementary knowledge we gain from other ancient Greek and Roman sources. After providing a vivid account of the agonizing nature of Jesus's sacrificial death, this chapter concludes by discussing Jesus's crucifixion as the greatest act in God's drama of redemption as well as our calling, as cross disciples, to not only behold his death but also to follow him and play our own parts in this drama.

Chapter 2 takes a close look at the seven sayings spoken by Jesus during his crucifixion. As I have said many times in the past, the seven last sayings of Jesus as he suffered on his cross represent the greatest sermon ever preached. More specifically, each of these sayings provides us with a different life principle that we need to adopt in order to become effective cross disciples. In this manner, this chapter demonstrates how Jesus's final words to humanity provide us a guide for how we need to think about our own crosses.

Chapter 3 examines the relationship between suffering and cross discipleship. Much like Jesus as he hung upon his cross, our mission as cross disciples will invite us to hang upon our own crosses and endure different degrees of suffering. In this chapter, we'll explore what we can learn from Jesus about what it means to "hang in there" and endure, or even embrace, the pain we encounter as we fulfill our cross duty. We'll also discover how the

Lord can use suffering to transform us and help us discover new freedom in Christ.

Chapter 4 shifts our focus to what the life of cross discipleship looks like as we grow in his grace and mercy. More specifically, this chapter presents what I call the U-A-O-Z Life model. Based upon the three groups of disciples discussed in 1 John 2:12–14, the U-A-O-Z Life model charts the progressive growth of the cross disciple from the *unbeliever* and *newborn* stages all the way to being a victorious and decorated *veteran warrior* of God's spiritual army. In doing so, this chapter provides a framework for helping us assess where each of us is on our own cross-carrying and cross-hanging journeys.

Chapter 5 looks at five particular experiences each of us will encounter as we ascend through the different stages of cross discipleship—*pain, gain, deign, reign,* and *remain.* As we will see in this chapter, it is through our *painful* experience of this fallen world that we seek out the incredible *gain* of our salvation. Next, it is through this *gain* that we begin to reach out to others as Jesus did and, in wisdom, *deign* the suffering that comes from our cross mission. Finally, it is only once we have learned to *deign* like Jesus that we can truly *reign* in this life as his cross disciples, as long as we continue to *remain* in the power of the Holy Spirit.

Finally, chapter 6 introduces three spiritual disciplines that are essential for each of us as we fulfill our duties as cross disciples—*praise, prayer,* and *passion.* As this chapter will illustrate, to truly flourish as we take up our cross and follow him, we must be propelled by *praise,* absorbed by *prayer,* and consumed by *passion* for God's desire and purposes. In doing so, we allow God to transform us into exactly who we were created to be.

CHAPTER 1

The Crucifixion of Jesus and the Drama of Redemption

I N ORDER TO UNDERSTAND THE cross that we are called to carry and hang upon, we must first start with our Lord's cross. After all, before we can commit to bearing our own cross, we need to have a good understanding of the meaning and purpose of Jesus's crucifixion as told in Scripture. It is only then that we can truly realize what it means to follow his imperative to take up our cross and follow him.

In this chapter, I will attempt to provide a summary of what we know historically about the crucifixion of Jesus, including his arrest, trials, and death. In doing so, my hope is that we might remember together in a more profound way the fantastic truth that we have been crucified with Christ, and we no longer live but Christ lives within us (Gal. 2:20). This will prepare us to think with more theological depth about his cross and ours in the following chapters. While I lack the space to offer an exhaustive treatment of Scripture, its historical context, and everything that has been written on the subject, my hope is that this brief survey will provide some thought-provoking perspectives on the significance of the crucifixion of Jesus Christ and guide us as we explore how his example leads us in our own cross-carrying mission.

From there, we will briefly reflect upon the crucifixion as the greatest act within God's "drama of redemption." We will discuss how we should not only contemplate the great mystery of Jesus's excruciating death but also strive to become transformed by his cross as participants in his salvific drama.

THE ARREST AND TRIALS OF JESUS

Our primary sources for understanding the specific events surrounding Jesus's crucifixion are the New Testament Gospels—Matthew, Mark, Luke, and John. While all four Gospels recount the arrest, trials, and execution of Jesus, each of them describes these events from different angles and with different theological emphases.

The arrest of Jesus and his trials before both the Jewish and Roman courts fail to conform to our modern legal notion of due process. This is egregiously witnessed in his arrest in the Garden of Gethsemane (Matt. 26:47–56; Mark 14:43–52; Luke 22:47–53; John 18:2–11). From the beginning, Jesus's arrest was suspect. He was not taken while committing a crime. He was arrested at night, even though he had been openly traveling around Jerusalem since he entered the city in a triumphant parade. He could easily have been arrested at any other time. His "accuser" was Judas, one of his own disciples who betrayed him. Finally, he was seized by a large crowd wielding swords, clubs, and torches. All of these armed men were sent by the chief priests to arrest one unarmed man who did not resist arrest.

The only violence that occurred during the entire incident was caused by Peter, one of Jesus's disciples (Matt. 26:51; Mark 14:47; John 18:10–11). In a hapless act of defense, Peter struck one of the high priest's servants with his sword and sliced off his ear (Matt. 26:51; Mark 14:47; Luke 22:50; John 18:10)! Immediately, Jesus took charge of his own arrest, giving the order that swords were unnecessary and then healing the man's ear. Indeed, Jesus went willingly and without a fight because this was God's plan according to Scripture, even though, as he told the crowd, he had a legion of angels ready to come to his defense (Matt. 26:53–54).

Following his arrest, the Gospels state that Jesus was taken before the Jewish high priest to be interrogated (Matt. 26:57–58; Mark 14:53–54; Luke 22:54–55; John 18:12–14, 19–24). After this initial interrogation, Jesus was brought before the Sanhedrin, the ruling assembly of Jewish elders in Jerusalem, to face trial. Unlike our modern judicial system, rules of proper evidence, the right to avoid self-incrimination, and the assumption of innocence until proven guilty were ignored or circumvented in Jesus's trial. According to the Gospel writers, neither the chief priests nor the Sanhedrin could find any evidence against Jesus, and the witnesses they called all gave false or contradictory testimonies (Matt. 26:59–60; Mark 14:55–59). Jesus remained silent throughout these accusations.

Finally, after some claimed that Jesus had threatened to destroy the temple, the high priest directly asked Jesus whether he was the Messiah, the Son of God (Matt. 26:62–63; Mark 14:60–61; Luke 22:67, 70). Jesus verified the high priest's statement, responding, "I am, and you will see the Son of Man sitting at the right hand of the Mighty One and coming on the clouds of heaven"

(Mark 14:62). Under Jewish law, it was *not* a crime to claim to be the Messiah, and claiming the title "Son of Man" was likely not considered criminal either. Nevertheless, in a rush to get this case to the Roman *praefectus* (provincial governor) Pontius Pilate early that morning, the Sanhedrin charged Jesus with blasphemy—a religious crime punishable by death according to Jewish law (Lev. 24:16; John 19:7).

Since the Sanhedrin did not have the power to execute Jesus on their own (John 18:31), the chief priests and elders had to bring him before Pilate to receive Roman authorization. In order to guarantee that Jesus would be put to death, the chief priests and elders presented Jesus as a criminal and lodged charges of sedition against him that suggested he was a threat to Roman rule. These accusations included that Jesus was subverting the Jews against Rome, that he opposed paying taxes to Caesar, and that he claimed to be the King of the Jews (Luke 23:2). But when Pilate questioned Jesus, the governor concluded that he was innocent of these charges (Luke 23:4; John 18:38).

Having learned that Jesus was from Galilee, Pilate next tried to transfer the entire mess to Herod Antipas, the Roman ruler of that region. Jesus and his accusers appeared before Herod, who had long wished to see Jesus in the hope of seeing a miracle. But like Pilate, Herod found no case against Jesus. After mocking Jesus by clothing Him in a king's finery, Herod and his soldiers sent Jesus back to Pilate (Luke 23:6–12).

Now, faced with making a decision at last and knowing that the chief priests had given Jesus over under false pretenses (Matt. 27:18; Mark 15:10), Pilate tried to appease the Jewish crowd by offering to release Jesus, as it was the tradition at Passover to release one prisoner to the Jews. But the crowd, stirred up by the chief priests, demanded that Pilate release the political prisoner, Barabbas, instead, and crucify Jesus (Matt. 27:20–22; Mark 15:11–13; Luke 23:18–21; John 18:40, 19:6). At first Pilate refused, telling the crowd again that Jesus had done nothing wrong. However, the crowds began to yell louder, and the Jewish leaders pressured Pilate to get the result they desired, threatening him that "If you let this man go, you are no friend of Caesar. Anyone who claims to be a king opposes Caesar" (John 19:12b).

Given Pilate's desire to maintain political order on behalf of his Roman superiors, sedition was a meaningful threat. So Pilate, the highest civil authority in Judea, sentenced Jesus to death by crucifixion for political rather than legal reasons. And thus, with a wry sense of humor, Pilate ordered that a placard detailing Jesus's crime appear atop His cross that read: "Jesus of Nazareth, the King of the Jews" (John 19:19).

CRUCIFIXION IN THE ROMAN WORLD

When Pilate sentenced Jesus to be crucified on the cross, he sent him to suffer an agonizing death. There has never been any form of execution invented on the face of the earth more cruel, shameful, or horrifying than crucifixion.

The English term "crucifixion" comes from the Latin word *crux*, which originally meant any large, upright stake used to impale or hang someone upon. Although the Romans perfected crucifixion as a painful form of execution, they did not invent it. Our earliest clear references to crucifixion identify it as a form of public execution used by the Persians. According to the ancient Greek

> There has never been any form of execution invented on the face of the earth more cruel, shameful, or horrifying than crucifixion.

historian Herodotus, the Persian emperor Darius the Great (ruled 522–486 BC) used crucifixion to punish various political prisoners. Other ancient peoples in the Mediterranean, such as the Greeks and the Carthaginians, would later use crucifixion at certain times as a mode of capital punishment. For example, Alexander the Great in 322 BC crucified all the men of military age from Tyre after successfully sieging the city. The Jews also practiced crucifixion on certain occasions. In 88 BC, the Jewish ruler Alexander Jannaeus crucified eight hundred Jews who had rebelled against him in front of their wives and children.

While other ancient peoples practiced crucifixion to some extent, it was the Romans who made it the preferred method for dealing with rebellious slaves, pirates, and other political criminals. The Romans crucified thousands upon thousands of individuals. For example, in 71 BC, the Roman army, led by the general Crassus, put down a slave rebellion led by the gladiator Spartacus. The Roman historian Appian writes that after Crassus captured the rebels, he crucified more than six thousand of the slaves alongside the road leading out of Rome. According to the Jewish historian Josephus, during the siege of Jerusalem in AD 70, the Romans crucified hundreds of Jews who attempted to escape, placing them right in front of the city walls so the remaining inhabitants could watch them suffer. As can be seen, public display was an important part of crucifixion, serving as a warning to anyone who might consider rebelling.

For the most part, Romans reserved crucifixion as a punishment for noncitizens and especially rebellious people of low status, including slaves, bandits, and foreigners. As a result, most of the people who were crucified had no guaranteed civil rights under Roman law. Those crucified included not only men but also women and, in some rare cases, children. In contrast, Roman citizens who were protected under civil law were almost always exempted from crucifixion as a form of capital punishment, since it was such a degrading death. Compare, for example, the traditions surrounding the martyrdoms of Peter and Paul in Rome. While Peter, a noncitizen, is said to have been crucified, Paul, a Roman citizen, is said to have been beheaded, a quicker and less denigrating form of capital punishment.

The Romans continued to use crucifixion as a mode of capital punishment long after Jesus's death, although by the third century AD, it seems to have become less common. However, it was not until the reign of Constantine the Great in the first half of the fourth century AD that crucifixion was finally banished throughout the Roman Empire. As the first Christian emperor, Constantine likely banned crucifixion both due to its brutality and in deference to Christ's crucifixion.

The fact that Jesus was sentenced to be crucified implies that he was viewed under Roman law as a lowly foreigner and a political enemy of the state. This can be confirmed by the references made of him during his trial as the "King of the Jews." Jesus was not murdered. He was legally executed in a manner consistent with the known practices of the time, even if Pontius Pilate did so as a form of political expediency.

7

The Crucifixion of Jesus

By dying on the cross, Jesus suffered arguably the most shameful and brutal mode of capital punishment ever invented by humankind, as several Roman writers living during that time acknowledged. For example, the Roman author Cicero said crucifixion was such a cruel and disgusting penalty that there were no words adequate enough to describe just how horrible it was. Crucifixion was not only excruciatingly painful but also very slow. Sometimes it could take several days before the person being crucified died.

Before being taken to the cross, Jesus was first subjected to scourging by the Roman soldiers (Matt. 27:26; Mark 15:15). This was not an uncommon practice for the Romans. Several ancient authors mention victims being flogged, beaten, or even burned before being crucified. The Roman author Seneca, for instance, mentions whips and other instruments of torture being used at crucifixions. The whips used to flog victims were made of several leather straps with nails, glass, or pieces of bone attached to the ends. As a result, scourging generally resulted in some degree of maiming with the skin cut into ribbons, sometimes even to the bone. Such injuries took their toll on the victim even before they were hung upon the cross.

After being scourged, Jesus was forced to carry his cross through the city (John 19:16–17). More specifically, Jesus probably had to carry the horizontal crossbeam (Latin: *patibulum*) of his cross, as the vertical beam (Latin: *stipes*) was likely already in the ground. Other Roman sources mention crucifixion victims having their arms stretched out and fastened to their *patibulum*, which they then had to carry out to the place of their execution. The crossbeam was often very heavy, sometimes weighing more than one hundred pounds. By this time in his crucifixion, Jesus was already so severely injured that he collapsed while carrying the crossbeam. The Gospels report that the soldiers forced a man from the crowd named Simon of Cyrene to carry the burden the rest of the way to the place of execution (Matt. 27:32; Mark 15:21; Luke 23:26).

Having reached Golgotha, a white stone outcropping that looked like a skull, Jesus was then crucified upon the cross. Before being uplifted on the cross, Jesus was attached to the crossbeam with nails (John 20:25). The Romans typically bound crucifixion victims to the crossbeam by their wrists, either by having them tied there with ropes, nailed in place, or both. The victim would then be lifted up as the crossbeam was attached to the upright stake, sometimes up to twelve feet above the ground.

In some cases, the victim's feet would also be nailed to the cross through their heel bones. We find evidence of this practice in the case of Yehohanan. In 1968, archaeologists discovered a rock-cut tomb on Mount Scopus near Jerusalem that belonged to a crucifixion victim named Yehohanan. When excavating the tomb, they discovered a four-inch nail still impaling Yehohanan's calcaneus bone in his right heel. As some ancient writers note, sometimes in addition to nailing the victim's feet, the Romans would also place a seat upon the cross, known as a *sedile*, to help support the bottom half of the victim. This was often done to make the crucifixion last even longer.

According to the Gospels, the Roman soldiers crucified Jesus between two thieves (Matt. 27:38; Mark 15:27; Luke 23:33–34; John 19:18). This was relatively normal since, as noted above, the Romans often crucified criminals in groups. During his crucifixion, Jesus's clothes were divided among the soldiers as plunder (Matt. 27:35; Mark 15:24; John 19:23–24). This is not surprising since people sentenced to death in ancient Rome lost the rights to their property.

Like most crucifixions, Jesus's execution took place in a public space and drew a crowd, including many who mocked Jesus as he died (Matt. 27:39–44; Mark 15:29–32; Luke 23:35–39). The Romans placed the placard Pilate had inscribed with the words "Jesus of Nazareth, the King of the Jews" atop the cross as well (Matt. 27:37; Mark 15:26; John 19:19–22). The use of a placard (known in Latin as a *titulus*) naming the crime for which someone was being executed is also mentioned in several other ancient sources.

Once upon the cross, Jesus experienced six hours of great agony. According to recent medical studies on the potential physical effects of crucifixion, asphyxiation is considered the ultimate cause of death for most victims, although hemorrhage, dehydration, shock, and cardiac arrest would have all played roles in the suffering they experienced. As the victim would hang with their arms extended, their respiratory muscles would become compromised, forcing them to push up against the cross in order to breathe. While pushing up would allow the victim to breathe, it was also incredibly painful to do so, as this placed pressure upon one's feet, which would be nailed to the cross. When this pain became too intense, the victim would slump down, transferring their weight back to their arms, which was also quite painful. This dreadful cycle would repeat itself until the person was exhausted or lapsed into unconsciousness, provided they had not already succumbed to their other injuries. Once they were unable to push up any longer, the victim would finally reach the point where their respiratory muscles would be essentially paralyzed. This, of course, would soon be followed by death.

Sometimes if the crucifixion process was taking too long, Roman soldiers would break the large bones in the legs of the victims to speed up the process. We see this in John 19:31–33 where the Jewish leaders petition Pilate to break the legs of Jesus and the thieves being crucified so that they could all be buried before the Passover Sabbath. However, John writes that when the soldiers came to Jesus, they found that he was already dead. To ensure that Jesus had died, the Roman soldiers used the most expedient method of assuring death by inserting a spear in his side, a much easier process than breaking his legs.

Once a crucifixion victim had died, the Romans sometimes allowed the body to be turned over to relatives or friends for burial according to local customs. This was the case with Jesus. According to the Gospels, a follower of Jesus named Joseph of Arimathea requested Jesus's body from Pilate and buried it in a rock-cut tomb before the start of the Sabbath (Matt. 27:57–60; Mark 15:42–47; Luke 23:50–56; John 19:38–42). Other times, however, the Romans would bury the bodies in a shallow grave, allowing them to be eaten by wild animals. And in war, during uprisings, or on other occasions of extreme public disorder, the Romans would often leave bodies on crosses for an extended period, serving as a grisly warning of what awaited those who defied Roman authority.

In summary, the historical record, medical insights, and archaeological discoveries mentioned above all cast more light on Jesus's crucifixion. While the New Testament Gospels give slightly different accounts of the crucifixion, a general picture still emerges that includes the following details. First, after his sentencing, Jesus was scourged by Roman soldiers. Then, Jesus was initially forced to carry his cross to the place of his execution. Once he collapsed due to the severity of his injuries, the Romans forced Simon of Cyrene to carry the crossbeam the rest of the way. Upon arriving at Golgotha, Jesus was then nailed to the crossbeam and lifted up on his cross. A placard identifying his crime was placed atop the cross, which was a normal practice. As he hung on the cross, Jesus was mocked and his belongings were divided among the soldiers. After dying, Jesus's side was pierced with a spear, and, finding him dead, the soldiers did not break his legs. Finally, Jesus's body was given to his friends for burial, which was not inconsistent with Roman custom.

The Drama of Redemption

Despite being an innocent man, Jesus was found guilty of blasphemy and sedition by the civil and religious authorities of his day. Jesus did not have a fair or lawful trial, at least by our standards. But by receiving a guilty verdict despite being innocent, Jesus identified with the guilt of our human rebellion against God's authority in Eden, as we see in Genesis 3. In the garden, Adam and Eve traded their innocence for guilt. In doing so, they sinned against God by blaspheming him and thereby received the appropriate sentence: death. They also offended God in a civil sense by stopping their work in the garden and hiding themselves, thereby receiving their appropriate punishment: banishment. In contrast, Jesus, the second Adam (2 Cor. 15:45), was entirely innocent but nevertheless judged guilty of both religious (blasphemy) and civil (sedition) crimes by the Jewish and Roman authorities. Only as an innocent man judged guilty could Jesus have been a sacrifice worthy enough to pay the penalty for humanity's rebellion in Eden and render us innocent once again before God's eyes.

The historical events surrounding Jesus's crucifixion described above were not random or accidental. Rather, they completed God's redemptive plan promised in Scripture, what we might call God's "drama of redemption," and made a way for human beings to escape the trap of sin the serpent sprang upon them in the garden. In the Old Testament, there are many texts that prophesy about the coming Messiah and his sacrificial death. One of the most evocative is Psalm 22:16–18:

> Dogs surround me,
> a pack of villains encircles me;
> they pierce my hands and my feet.
> All my bones are on display;
> people stare and gloat over me.
> They divide my clothes among them
> and cast lots for my garment.

Isaiah 53 also speaks of the fate of the Suffering Servant who was "despised and rejected by mankind, a man of suffering, and familiar with pain . . . pierced for our transgressions" (Isa. 53:3, 5). Jesus himself even prophesized before his crucifixion that he would face this agonizing fate in Mark 10:32–34:

> They [Jesus and the disciples] were on their way up to
> Jerusalem, with Jesus leading the way, and the disciples

were astonished, while those who followed were afraid. Again he took the Twelve aside and told them what was going to happen to him. "We are going up to Jerusalem," he said, "and the Son of Man will be delivered over to the chief priests and the teachers of the law. They will condemn him to death and will hand him over to the Gentiles, who will mock him and spit on him, flog him and kill him. Three days later he will rise."

As he suffered his arrest, trials, severe beating, and execution, Jesus knew he was obediently following the Father's foretold eternal plan of reconciliation and redemption for the fallen, helpless people he created and loved! When Jesus died upon the cross, his destiny and mission were all fulfilled.

Without question, the crucifixion of Jesus was the single most important event ever beheld throughout history. One of my favorite Greek words from the New Testament is the verb *theaomai*, the same word from which we get our English word "theater." There is not a single word in English that possesses the exact meaning as *theaomai*. It is often translated as "to look at," "to watch," or "to behold" in our Bibles, but it also has the meaning "to discern," "to gaze upon," or "to contemplate" by sight. For example, when the apostle John uses the verb in his statement that "we beheld [*etheasametha*] his glory, the glory as of the only begotten of the Father" (John 1:14 KJV), he is claiming that those who witnessed Jesus didn't just *see* him but were also *moved* and *overwhelmed with his significance* as they began to *intensely contemplate* all he was as God in the flesh! In other words, to truly see the Messiah—to "theaterize" him—means to behold him in careful contemplation, to closely study him and be overwhelmed by his significance, and to allow him to become our greatest reality.

When we expectantly and attentively behold the Savior upon the cross and attend "the theater of God" in Scripture, we become captured by the greatest drama of

> Without question, the crucifixion of Jesus was the single most important event ever beheld throughout history.

all time—the life, mission, message, crucifixion, and resurrection of Jesus. We have front-row seats to the drama of redemption starring the Messiah himself in the leading role. And it is the crucifixion of Jesus, as recounted in the New Testament, that represents the most compelling scene in this drama. To truly behold those six hours that the Savior hung in excruciating pain on the cross involves so much more than simply reading the words about his arrest, trials, and crucifixion. We must theaterize the crucifixion of Jesus in Scripture by fully seeing him upon the cross and hearing the life-changing words from his Spirit in order for the drama of redemption to stir our hearts.

Of course, the fact that it was necessary for the Father to send God in the flesh—the Messiah Jesus—so that he could be rejected by humanity and endure the deprivations, hardships, evil, hurts, humiliations, and limitations of our fallen world is a mystery that is far beyond our comprehension. As Paul writes, the message of God's drama of redemption that we declare is "a mystery that has been hidden and that God destined for our glory before time began" (1 Cor. 2:7). However, it is through our relationship with Jesus that this great mystery has now been disclosed to us as God's people (Col.1:26). Even still, the crucifixion of Jesus is so mysterious, so profound, and so beyond human understanding that even through the revealing touch of the Holy Spirit, we are only able to get a glimpse of the purposes and promises of God's drama of redemption for our fallen condition.

However, we are called to do more than simply *behold* the crucifixion of our Savior and *theaterize* him hanging upon his cross—we are also called to *participate* in God's drama of redemption. When we truly become absorbed in God's drama of redemption, we become assigned by God to play our own small parts as his cross disciples! The cross of Christ must not only be powerfully perceived but must also be personally pursued and prayerfully practiced if we are to follow Jesus in the way he commanded so that we might glorify the Father and impact others. As Jesus commands in Luke 9:23, a verse we saw in the introduction and will encounter many other times in this book: "Whoever wants to be my disciple must deny themselves and take up their cross daily and follow me." Once we authentically contemplate Jesus's crucifixion, his cross mission will begin to dominate our thoughts, motives, hopes, and actions. It is then, when our ardent ambition, aspiration, and agenda are centered on possessing the mind, heart, vision, and will of Messiah Jesus, that we can embrace the cross he has personally assigned us and play our part in his redemptive drama.

DURING HIS TRIALS, ARREST, AND crucifixion, Jesus experienced excruciating pain, as we discover in the New Testament Gospels and find confirmed by our historical knowledge of crucifixion in the ancient world. On the cross, the Lord Jesus gave his *best* as he endured the *worst* agony ever suffered by humanity. Through the mysterious wonder of the Messiah's love, he brought redemption and restoration for all of creation, including the human beings who crucified him. Just as all of humanity is guilty for his death, so also Jesus died for all of humanity. However, the significance of Jesus's cross does not stop there. From his *best* sacrifice and *worst* suffering we can also discover our *most* for living abundantly and fulfilling completely his intentions for our cross discipleship. In this manner, Jesus's crucifixion not only delivers us from sin but also demonstrates what it looks like for us to embrace his commandment to follow him and take up our cross daily. Just as our Savior did, we too must seek to discover, accept, carry, and endure the cross we have been assigned, regardless of whatever may confront or befall us!

Throughout the rest of this book, we'll explore in greater theological detail how Jesus's crucifixion—including the words he spoke on the cross and the way he died there—should shape how we understand and act out our parts as cross disciples in God's redemptive drama. Tragically, however, even the greatest of all theater performances is lost on those who never attend. Before we can become cross disciples, we must first behold and authentically contemplate for ourselves the mystery of Jesus's cross as witnessed in Scripture. It is then that we can begin to fulfill the mission to which we have been called—to become cross disciples in all the moments he gives us upon this earth.

QUESTIONS FOR REFLECTION

1) Why is Jesus's crucifixion so important for understanding our own cross-carrying missions?

2) What are one or two facts you learned in this chapter about Jesus's arrest, trials, and crucifixion that you didn't know prior to reading this book? How did this historical look at Jesus's death change how you understand his cross?

3) How would you define God's "drama of redemption"? How does this idea change the way you approach how Scripture portrays Jesus's crucifixion?

4) What does it mean for us to play our "small parts" in God's "drama of redemption"? What are some potential examples of what this might look like in your own life?

CHAPTER 2

Jesus's Last Words from the Cross

AS I MENTIONED AT THE end of the previous chapter, Jesus's crucifixion was without question the greatest scene in God's drama of redemption. It was on the cross that his mindset reached its climax and was revealed to humankind; he knew he was fulfilling the Father's eternal plan of reconciliation, redemption, and resurrection for the fallen and helpless people he loved. As Christians, we are called to "theaterize" this mysterious scene by taking our front-row seats, intensely contemplating his sacrifice as witnessed in Scripture, and absorbing ourselves in God's drama so that we can play our own parts as cross disciples. And it is our Messiah Jesus who was chosen by the Father to play the lead role in this eternal drama.

Theaterizing the crucifixion involves more than just beholding the agonizing suffering of Jesus. We must also take to heart the life-changing words he uttered on that day. While the New Testament Gospels preserve many wonderful things Jesus Christ said during his earthly ministry, the seven last sayings he proclaimed during his crucifixion are especially powerful (see Figure 1). These seven sayings are perhaps the most intense, essential, and profound statements he ever made, revealing his mind and heart of love.

Figure 1: The Seven Last Sayings of Jesus

Saying	Scripture Quotation	Action
1	"Father, forgive them, for they do not know what they are doing." (Luke 23:34)	Forgiving
2	"Truly I tell you, today you will be with me in paradise." (Luke 23:43)	Ministering
3	To Mary, "Woman, here is your son," and to the beloved disciple, "Here is your mother." (John 19:26–27)	Remembering
4	"My God, my God, why have you forsaken me?" (Matt. 27:46; Mark 15:34)	Seeking
5	"I am thirsty." (John 19:28)	Suffering
6	"It is finished." (John 19:30)	Finishing
7	"Father, into your hands I commit my spirit." (Luke 23:46)	Trusting

I've said many times throughout the last fifty years that the seven sayings uttered by our Messiah while he hung upon his cross may be the greatest sermon ever preached! Indeed, I believe that this message from the cross was the most powerful utterance ever made from human lips because our Lord purposely and painfully bled for the whole world while he made them. Each of these seven statements reflects a central theological aspect of Jesus's life and ministry.

I believe that each of these seven sayings reveals to us a key life principle of eternal fulfillment for our brief walk on earth. These seven principles are forgiving, ministering, remembering, seeking, suffering, finishing, and trusting. As I'll show in this chapter, each of these deep life principles, embodied by Jesus on his cross, must be branded on our minds, hearts, and wills as we carry and hang upon our

> The seven sayings uttered by our Messiah while he hung upon his cross may be the greatest sermon ever preached.

own crosses. Incarnating these seven attitudes must be the highest priority of our daily lives! When we can say these seven things—and authentically mean them—as we seek to do Christ's will in our lives, we spiritually come ever closer to the Savior's cross and our own that he has planned for us.

The Seven Last Sayings

The last words uttered by the Lord while he hung in agony for six hours contain, without any doubt, the most magnificent sacrificial message of redemptive love and conquering hope ever revealed throughout creation. We find these seven sayings scattered across the crucifixion accounts of the New Testament Gospels.

Always Forgiving
The first saying is found in Luke: "Father, forgive them, for they do not know what they are doing" (Luke 23:34). This statement is

found only in Luke's Gospel. Jesus says this right after he is lifted up upon the cross as his clothing is being divided up by the soldiers. We cannot lightly pass over the horror of what the religious leaders and political rulers were doing to Jesus. Yet, even the pre-crucifixion beating and the agony they inflicted on him on the cross could not block the love he continued to have for them. Amazing! We could paraphrase Luke 23:34 as the Lord announcing to both those responsible for his unjust death and to all of humanity: "They are helpless. I forgive their unforgivable sins."

Forgiveness is the only path for the loving heart of the Godhead to offer reconciliation and redemption to the world. According to Paul, upon the cross "God was reconciling the world to himself in Christ, not counting people's sins against them" (2 Cor. 5:19a). What incredible words! All of us sin big and continually fail, which means that forgiveness from God is urgent so that crazed, rebellious, and demented humankind might become reconciled with him. To paraphrase the words of the psalmist, no one can survive his or her sins, but with the Lord, there is forgiveness (Ps. 130:3–4). Similarly, in Hebrews, the Holy Spirit testifies that "I will put my laws in their hearts, and I will write them on their minds" so that "Their sins and lawless acts I will remember no more" (Heb. 10:15–18).

Such words of forgiveness are the first thing we ought to say to anyone who has hurt us. Many years ago, I used to say that people who wronged me just *didn't know what they were doing!* I would often smile to myself at their foolishness as I forgave them! I have since come to repentantly realize (and humbly confess) that, without the Spirit's guidance, *I often don't know what I'm doing either!* I'm just as ignorant, dense, and blind as anyone else, since I, too, depend too readily on my flawed mind and fleshly nature.

Because the Savior is wondrously open to forgiving *everything* that sinful people (including me) do, I should have that same forgiveness in my mind and heart as well. It is only then that I can receive Christ's power to forgive myself and experience the depth of the Savior's love.

The Lord was *always forgiving*—even to those who unforgivably crucified him—and we should follow his example. We must always love people for what they can become and not focus on their weaknesses and sins. We must conquer our human blindness and self-worship and learn to forgive as the Lord has forgiven us (Col. 3:31; Eph. 4:32). The life-changer, of course, is to humbly remember our own experience of forgiveness from our Savior. Remember always that Christ has done much more for you than the many sins you have committed against him, others, and yourself. His forgiveness exceeds all your faults! Please prayerfully ponder 1 John 4:9–21:

> This is how God showed his love among us: He sent his one and only Son into the world that we might live through him. This is love: not that we loved God, but that he loved us and sent his Son as an atoning sacrifice for our sins. Dear friends, since God so loved us, we also ought to love one another. No one has ever seen God; but if we love one another, God lives in us and his love is made complete in us.
>
> This is how we know that we live in him and he in us: He has given us of his Spirit. And we have seen and testify that the Father has sent his Son to be the Savior of the world. If anyone acknowledges that Jesus is the

Son of God, God lives in them and they in God. And so we know and rely on the love God has for us.

God is love. Whoever lives in love lives in God, and God in them. This is how love is made complete among us so that we will have confidence on the day of judgment: In this world we are like Jesus. There is no fear in love. But perfect love drives out fear, because fear has to do with punishment. The one who fears is not made perfect in love.

We love because he first loved us. Whoever claims to love God yet hates a brother or sister is a liar. For whoever does not love their brother and sister, whom they have seen, cannot love God, whom they have not seen. And he has given us this command: Anyone who loves God must also love their brother and sister.

The great guilt you feel in your heart is wiped away by the greater love and forgiveness Jesus feels in his heart for you. In response, we must learn how to be always forgiving—even for those who are unforgivable—to please our Father. Taking up, carrying, and enduring your cross means *always forgiving* others. Forgive as you are forgiven!

Always Ministering

The second saying spoken by Jesus during his crucifixion appears in Luke 23:43, which again is the only Gospel that records this saying. According to Luke, when one of the guilty thieves crucified alongside Jesus began to insult him, the other thief rebuked his fellow criminal, declaring that Jesus had done no wrong. Then he said to Jesus, "Jesus, remember me when you come into your kingdom" (Luke 23:42). Jesus responded to him by saying, "Truly I tell you, today you will be with me in paradise" (Luke 23:43).

This brief exchange is loaded with several great applications, but one action stands out. Regardless of the horrendous agony Jesus was experiencing, he still reached out to another suffering person! With the authority and love of the Father, Jesus ministered to that sinful, crucified criminal when he called on him for help. Jesus always recognized that people needed him and, regardless of their circumstances, acted as a servant to them, if he felt it was the Father's will and they were repentant of heart (Luke 22:27). He selflessly served them by sharing the Father's message of love, truth, deliverance, and redemption, even as he was dying upon the cross. As the Good Shepherd, Jesus Christ laid down his life for all his sheep, continuously ministering to them to bring them closer to himself (John 10:11, 17:13–24).

During my years serving as the chaplain for the Arkansas Razorbacks football team, I would meet with the players every Thursday night at nine o'clock. As my wife, Shirley, could tell you, some of those Thursday nights I was so dead, so beat, so whipped from my many other ministry duties that I didn't care if I went or not! But we had a deal, so I showed up. And as I would drive over to campus, feeling completely exhausted, I'd say in the car, "Lord, I have no idea what I'm going to say tonight." So I would ask God to help me through it, praying that he'd strengthen me one more time. Many times I would remember the words of 2 Timothy 1:7 as I drove: "For the Spirit God gave us does not make us timid, but gives us power, love and self-discipline." And sure enough, every time I would minister to those players, I would have such energy that they would have thought I'd been waiting two years to get there! In those moments when I could see God becoming real to them through me, my whole life changed!

Truly, there is nothing on earth more fulfilling and wonderful than seeing God ministering to others through you and watching others embrace the Savior as the Lord of their lives. Every one of us has it in us—a parent with their young child, a college student with their peers, a cadet with their captain, an employee with their coworker, or anyone else. You don't have to be a preacher to have God work through you and touch others. All you have to do is trust him with boldness and, in the words of 2 Timothy 1:7, accept his power and love.

No matter how inadequate we might feel or how much we are hurting personally, we can still seek to express the grace, love, and truth of God to others (as we are spiritually able) and trust his promises. As I was once told as a young minister, "The only thing we can do is do our best and leave the rest." We can still bring other people blessing even in the midst of our own tension and agony.

The Lord was *always ministering*, not just during his earthly ministry but even in the painful moments before his death. In the Gospels, we witness Jesus acting as a servant among his disciples by washing their feet (John 13:4) and instructing them that "whoever wants to become great among you must be your servant . . . just as the Son of Man did not come to be served, but to serve, and to give his life as a ransom for many" (Matt. 20:26–27). Great honor and authority are reserved for the disciple who has the heart of a servant. In whatever way our Savior could serve others while he was on this earth, he did so in order that they could know the Father, overcome their problems, and conquer their inevitable battles. In the same way, we too, as cross disciples, should continuously seek out ways to minister to others.

Even today, from a minor concern to a major crisis, Jesus will always prove himself sympathetic and sufficient. This means that taking up, carrying, and enduring your cross also means *always ministering* like our Lord. Care for others! Know God's message of life and hope and make it lovingly clear for others. Make time to serve everyone you can.

Always Remembering

The third saying concerns the Lord's compassion for his mother as she endured the emotional devastation of watching him suffer and die. According to the Gospel of John, the only Gospel in which this comment appears, when Jesus saw Mary at the cross alongside his beloved disciple, he said to her, "Dear woman, here is your son" before telling his disciple, "Here is your mother" (John 19:26–27 NLT).

Jesus knew the shattering pain and grief within his mother's heart. To her, he was still her little boy! She remembered the miraculous announcement of his conception, the trip to the stable, his birth in Bethlehem, the angels, and his childhood in Nazareth. She remembered him playing as a boy, when he went missing in the temple, and watching him grow into a young man. She remembered his claims of messiahship as well as his miracles and healings. And as she remembered him, so he remembered her! On the cross, Jesus remembered his bond with his mother along with his calling and mission in her life.

Jesus always sees everything, no matter what the pain is, and that's what makes a great mother or father. Looking back at my childhood, my mother was always aware of my pain and my needs. How about that? I didn't always know that she was, and I didn't always care that she was, but she was always mindful when I was suffering. Even when our Lord was enduring tremendous pain, he still looked with compassion at his mother. He knew that she would no longer be his mother, that their relationship was never going to be the same, and that she was experiencing tremendous grief and loss. When he looked at the beloved disciple and presented him to Mary, Jesus showed that he was aware of her pain and needs. He supplied his mother with a new son and thus remembered his duty to his family.

Jesus never forgot his mother in her moment of abject grief and emotional need, and he does the same for us as well! In doing so, Jesus modeled how we need to take care of our loved ones. No matter what struggle you might be facing, it is important to remain truthful and compassionate to your mother or father, your husband or wife, your children or grandchildren, your in-laws or friends, just as our Lord was to his mother on the cross. No matter how good or bad things may be going, we must always keep our family and friends in our mind, be aware of their pain, and seek to meet the needs of everyone the Holy Spirit directs us to. This isn't always easy. At certain times, some relationships may create more needs than they meet. In those moments, we have to radically trust God to meet our needs so that we can strive to meet the needs of others. In those moments, we must let the spirit of Christ work in us, the same Christ who showed compassion to his earthly family in his moment of final suffering.

What we owe our families and loved ones (especially our mothers) should never be forgotten and should always be a priority, no matter what the occasion or the circumstances. The Lord was *always remembering* those whom he loved, even in his painful final moments, and we should be exactly like him by remembering those we love in life when we take up, carry, and endure our cross. Remembering those to whom we are debtors and admirers is perhaps one of the deepest, richest, and most lingering and moving experiences of our lives. To remember others in love will always mobilize and ignite our hearts and bring gratitude and praise to our minds.

Remembering is the Godhead's gift that enables us to see our life in the enormity of his creation. Like Jesus, never forget your duty to the loved ones the Father has given you. Be sure to express your gratitude to those who love you by taking the initiative and serving them consistently.

Always Seeking

The fourth saying has to be one of the most awesome and mysterious sayings Jesus ever spoke: "My God, my God, why have you forsaken me?" This is found in Matthew 27:46 and Mark 15:34. Apart from the hints of divine revelation provided by Scripture and the Holy Spirit, the profound, eternal insight of this saying is far beyond our human understanding.

Although we could go in many different theological and philosophical directions, the bottom line, to me, is this: The Father, compelled by his redemptive love, determined to complete his eternal plan by sending Jesus to the cross, letting him die horrendously, and refusing to save him from his sacrificial mission. As a result, our Messiah in his humanity was troubled with grief and anxiety in his heart and cried out for more understanding, "My God, my

God, why? I am abandoned! Forsaken by you! Left alone! You have turned your back on me!" Yet, as Hebrews 12:2 states, "For the joy set before him he endured the cross." Even when experiencing death and despair on the cross, the Lord Jesus was *always seeking* the Father, the ultimate answer to all things and the revealer of all things. Jesus never stopped seeking to understand the mysteries of his Father's love, his truth, his purposes, and his glory.

Seeking the will of his Father, Jesus understood that the cross was his calling as the Son of Man and that when he left this earth and returned to his Father, he would know all things. Thus, Jesus did not ask the Father to save him from this hour, because it was for this very purpose that he came to earth: to obediently glorify the name of his Father (John 12:23–33). Jesus put the Father first in everything. As Hebrews 5:7–9 states:

> During the days of Jesus' life on earth, he offered up prayers and petitions with fervent cries and tears to the one who could save him from death, and he was heard because of his reverent submission. Son though he was, he learned obedience from what he suffered and, once made perfect, he became the source of eternal salvation for all who obey him.

The eternal will of God always trumps the temporary actions of mankind! Be sure that God's will is anchored within your mind and heart.

When suffering, hardship, loss, and tragedy come into our lives, it is never wrong to ask God why. After all, even Jesus in his humanity asked why while he agonized on the cross! When we brokenly ask the Father to give us his answer, we can be sure that our seeking will be rewarded for *our good* and *his glory*. Our questions will always be heard by God, and their answers will be revealed, if we keep searching for him and stop following the desires of our sinful selves. Yet, only in heaven will all of our questions be answered.

For now, taking up our cross is more urgent than knowing *why* the Lord wants us to take it up. We must act in obedience, just as our Savior did. We must put God first in everything. It is when we follow him in joy as we carry our cross that we will experience the Godhead's grace of love and reality of truth! In the words of Paul, "join with me in suffering for the gospel, by the power of God" (2 Tim. 1:8b). Adjusting to the Father's will rather than your sinful self turns your *worst* into his *most*, which becomes your *best*. When we advance in Christ, we begin to maturely pursue and resolve the confusing and critical conflict between sin and righteousness on this fallen earth.

Taking up, carrying, and enduring your cross means *always seeking* the Father first in all things, knowing that all the answers you really need to your questions are found in the Father's grace and truth.

Always Suffering

The fifth saying, found only in John 19:28, is when Jesus told the soldiers, "I am thirsty." The Savior was in the perfect will of God, accomplishing the greatest event the Father ever decreed for the earth, but he still experienced human fatigue, exhaustion, pain, emptiness, and rejection. The Lord was *always suffering* to advance the Father's will. To paraphrase Hebrews 5:8, even though Jesus was the Father's one and only Son, he still learned obedience through what he suffered!

The Messiah understood that sacrifice was needed and deep pain was to be expected as he strove to live for his Father's truth. Jesus saw that there was no greater need for mankind than to receive God's grace of love, reality of truth, and perfect will. His suffering obedience to his Father should be our own answer and intent for living. Jesus had to experience the emptiness of human rejection, endure the madness and duplicity of a world in rebellion, and withstand the desperate dimness and grief of being alone as he suffered and emptied himself as a sacrifice on the cross. As Jesus the Savior himself said, "The Son of Man must suffer many things" (Luke 9:22a).

Here we encounter the great mystery of human evil and righteous suffering. I spent a year of my doctoral study in a seminar focused on evil and suffering. My short answer from that experience is this: We must trust God to use suffering in this fallen world for our good and his greater glory. We must stay in praise, learn our painful lessons, and wait on his purposes and resolutions. I am convinced that in the fullness of time, the Godhead will triumph over evil so that it will no longer abuse his creation. But until then, the Godhead allows suffering to give his chosen people *greater training* in the glory of godliness. He turns evil's *abuse* for his *use* and then will *refuse* evil a place in his heavenly creation!

Taking up, carrying, and enduring your cross calls for you to be *always suffering* according to the Father's will, just like Jesus did. As Paul writes, "For it has been granted to you on behalf of Christ not only to believe in him, but also to suffer for him" (Phil. 1:29). We also read in 1 Peter, "Therefore, since Christ suffered in the flesh, equip yourselves also with the same resolve—because the one who suffered in the flesh has finished with sin" (1 Peter 4:1 HCSB). None of us will accomplish the deepest will of God without, at times, paying a costly price from the malignant evil of the fall while

> We must trust God to use suffering in this fallen world for our good and his greater glory.

seeking to obey and yield to our Messiah's call. No one escapes the suffering involved in living in this fallen world.

Yet, even your afflictions can reveal his greater purposes and promises as well as the realization that we can live in triumph in the midst of satanic conflict. We can therefore, in the words of Paul, rejoice in our suffering knowing that his unstoppable love never stops working toward good in our lives (Rom. 5:3). And we have the promise of the Savior from John 16:33: "I have told you these things, so that in me you may have peace. In this world you will have trouble. But take heart! I have overcome the world."

Always Finishing

The sixth saying spoken by Jesus appears only in John 19:30 where, after receiving a drink, Jesus said, "It is finished." The English phrase "It is finished" is only one word in Greek (*tetelestai*), which can mean finished, completed, done, or perfected. For a while I thought that Jesus whispered this, but now I believe that this was shouted out loud by the Savior! Things weren't totally finished here on the Savior's cross, as his resurrection, ascension, and the gift of the Holy Spirit were still to come. And still today we await his return and the final judgment to commence in the Godhead's total redemption drama. But what the Savior had completed in his dying moments was *the crucifixion part* of his messianic mission. Despite his suffering and agony, Jesus knew he must continue on and complete his earthly assignment as directed and empowered by the Father.

I have now finished more than ninety years of my earthly mission as a *first-birth human* in the flesh and more than seventy years as a *second-birth new creation* in Christ. I remain increasingly grateful, expectant, and content as I strive to complete my current cross mission as I have received it from the Master. I sense I'm probably close to my final ministry assignment as I experience my "sunset decade" of old age—the glory of my veteran years. We need to remember that old age is God's idea, and God doesn't have any bad ideas. Above all, I want to finish my little life well in a way pleasing to him! As my body weakens, however, I'm also experiencing my "awakening dawn" era of life in the Spirit! I'm actually living out one of my favorite and most impactful memory verses from 1951:

> Therefore we do not give up. Even though our outer person is being destroyed, our inner person is being renewed day by day. For our momentary light affliction is producing for us an absolutely incomparable eternal weight of glory. So we do not focus on what is seen, but on what is unseen. For what is seen is temporary, but what is unseen is eternal (2 Cor. 4:16–18 HCSB).

When I first memorized those verses, I had only been a Christian for eighteen months and was experiencing my first dark night of the soul. I was so discouraged that I felt ready to give up. But these verses gave me strength. In fact, no other passage in Scripture has sustained me in my doubts, depressions, and despairs more than these three verses! I'm seeing the Lord more clearly. I'm feeling him more nearly. I'm loving him more dearly.

Taking up, carrying, and enduring your cross means being like our Lord Jesus who was *always finishing* his Father's directives. Like Jesus on the cross, we, too, should continually seek to finish our own progressive parts of our Father's mission. He will tell us what, where, when, why, whence, and how if we ask him and are living for his cross intentions. We must continue in his Word (John 8:31), continue in his love (John 15:9), and continue with Christ in our trials (Luke 22:28). Let us be content to finish the current thing and then continue toward the next challenge the Holy Spirit puts before us! Everything he has called you to do he has also given you the power to do. All that matters is learning his love and promises for your greatest finish.

Always Trusting

The seventh and final saying is found only in Luke 23:46. There, the Gospel states that before taking his final breath, Jesus called out in a loud voice, "Father, into your hands I commit my spirit." What is so perfect, profound, and powerful here is that just as the Savior began these seven final statements by calling on the Father in prayer to forgive those who were crucifying him, so too he ends these seven sayings in a prayer of commitment to the Father. Just as Jesus began and ended with the Father, we should do the same as cross disciples.

The Savior trusted that everything about his past, present, and future—especially his six agonizing and grueling hours on the cross—was in the loving hands of the Father. In the words of Job, "Though he slay me, yet I will trust in him!" (Job 13:15a KJV). Our Messiah was "slain" by the Father to inaugurate his salvific drama of redemption. Jesus knew his Father reigned and that he had to trust his Father while disregarding the world's affliction, attacks, rejections, humiliations, and deceits. The Lord Jesus trusted that his obedience would honor and bless the Father with the highest acclaim throughout eternity (Phil. 2:6–11). This trust in the Father empowered our Messiah Jesus to handle everything on earth with confidence, turning all his suffering trials into significant triumphs. Even his crucifixion and death became his resurrection and exaltation (John 12:23–26, 16:33).

Taking up, carrying, and enduring your cross means *always trusting* God, just as Jesus Christ trusted his Father regardless of the circumstances. As I have sought to trust the Father in my life, the words of Psalm 31:4–8 have constantly liberated me from all the empty lies and futile hindrances of earth. It has become one of my most precious life passages through which the Holy Spirit's words have continually restored me. Please hear a paraphrase of these verses in my own words:

> Free me from the earthen traps set for me,
> from the sins of others, the demonic lies, and the
> blind foolishness of my own skewed heart!
> For you, my Master, are my only refuge and escape!
> Into your hands I commit my spirit!
> Redeem me by your truth from the deceits,
> diminishments, and damage of this fallen earth.
> O Lord, my God,

I praise you for leading me out of my affliction and anguish and giving me a life in the spacious beauty and reconciliation wholeness of your grace (love) and truth (reality).

Learning to truly trust the Father's promises, plans, and purposes is the guaranteed key to the peace that surpasses all understanding. We are all ignorant, dense, and arrogant fools when we do not put our lives fully in the Father's hands. When trusting the Father means everything to our lives, all other things are conquered by his solving, resolving, and absolving. Having faith in our God in everything we experience is our highest life decision, reward, and comfort—all things are conquered, all lessons learned! Trusting his love is of the highest significance!

However, cross-carrying faith means more than simply believing and trusting in God; it also means *striving to do what he wills*. The cross disciple is the Christian who aims to discover their cross and be crucified upon it, trusting what the Lord directs them to do.

While dying on the cross, the Lord Jesus didn't speak five or eight random thoughts at the spur of the moment. Instead, he gave us exactly seven statements—a holy number—that we need to explore and take to heart as we follow him daily by taking up our crosses. When he conquered his cross, Jesus addressed human blindness and sin by being the *always forgiving Savior*. He offered his presence and comfort as the *always ministering Shepherd*. He provided for the needs of those he loved by being the *always re-membering Son of Man*. He obediently sought out his Father by being the *always seeking Servant*. He experienced agony and thirst as the *always suffering Redeemer*. He completed his earthly mission as the *always finishing Messiah*. Finally, he committed himself to the Father as the *always trusting Son of God*.

Jesus has conquered his cross, but our cross mission is only beginning. Revelation 14:4b reads, "They follow the Lamb wherever he goes." In our case, "wherever" certainly means going to the cross!

Again, in my view, our Lord's last words from the cross represent what is probably the greatest sermon ever preached! These seven sayings encompass all there is to know about the meaning of our creation, rebellion, redemption, and destiny as well as the assurances that we have found and possess in Messiah Jesus. The deepest problem with many of us who claim to be the Master's followers and attempt to take up our crosses is that there is little, if any, *cross blood* on *us*. The Savior *suffered* and *bled* upon the cross while he *preached* his last words. In the words of Paul, he "fought the good fight"—in Greek literally "agonized the good agony"—and nobly endured (2 Tim. 4:7). But *preaching* is often the only thing we actually do! So frequently we lead an empty or weak cross life that cannot empower our words. Until we learn and practice *how* and *what* it means to *bleed* for the Father's intentions, we will experience mostly self-centered, insignificant, and squandered lives. We will live cross-less lives. Our hearts must truly long for his presence, his purposes, his paths, and his pleasures (Ps. 16:5–11)!

Living as cross disciples and playing our part in the drama of redemption must be a continuous, earnest, and sacrificial daily quest! The more perfectly we learn to continually take up our own cross—whether we are bleeding or not at the time—the more effective the Father's plan will be when it comes to reaching and serving the people in our world. As we saw above, when we "theaterize" Jesus's final words, which were spoken as he endured the torture and humiliation of hanging on his cross, we can begin to contemplate the connection between his crucifixion and our own hanging on the cross. It is only when we authentically hear and act upon these seven sayings that we can start to comprehend the implications of repeating Christ's life by taking up our own cross on a daily basis, if not a moment-by-moment basis.

> Until we learn and practice *how* and *what* it means to *bleed* for the Father's intentions, we will experience mostly self-centered, insignificant, and squandered lives.

In conclusion, I believe that each of us must recognize three possible conditions before following Jesus as cross disciples. First, each of us must eagerly strive to be cross mastered by the Master. Second, we must each recognize that we are mostly ignorant of what it truly means to carry our cross daily and must commit ourselves anew to cross learning so that we can more precisely follow the Master. Third, even though we may be able to recognize and appreciate all that Jesus has done for us, when it comes to sacrificing ourselves and being mastered by his cross, we may still be fearful or immaturely hesitant. Therefore, all of us, no matter our condition, should pray the following prayer daily:

My dear Messiah Savior,

I know I am too much of a weak, foolish, dense, and distracted disciple!

I do want my life to count to my maximum for your honor and your people.

May I add to your glory by bleeding for others.

May I destroy my old self by taking up the cross actions you give me.

I humbly, devotedly, and urgently ask you to teach me how to *bleed for you as you bled for me*!

QUESTIONS FOR REFLECTION

1) Why are the last words that Jesus spoke upon the cross "the greatest sermon ever preached"? What makes these sayings so powerful?

2) What are the seven life principles that Jesus preached upon the cross?

3) Pick one of the seven principles discussed above. How do Jesus's words and actions model how we should embrace that principle in our own cross-carrying lives?

4) Think of some practical ways a cross disciple might apply these seven principles to their lives. How would these principles change the way you think about and act upon your personal calling to cross discipleship?

CHAPTER 3

Suffering and Cross Discipleship

T O BE HONEST, I WISH I could say that I first received the inspiration for this chapter when I was studying the biblical Greek or Hebrew, or that the Lord suddenly appeared to me in my study and gave me some sort of grand revelation. The truth is that this message first came to me one day when I noticed a poster hanging on the wall. On this poster there was a little kitten dangling from a tree limb, his front claws barely latched onto the branch above as his body swung down below. Underneath the dangling cat were three words: *Hang in there.*

When I first saw that poster, I said to myself, *Boy, that's my life. How many times have I felt like I was just barely hanging in there? How many times have I felt like my prayers, my actions, my friends, and my scheming weren't doing me any good? How many times have I felt like I couldn't find counsel anywhere, and all I could do was hang in there and suffer?*

All of us can point to times in life when we felt that we could barely "hang in there" any longer, that there was nothing we could do to help ourselves, that it was hopeless to try, or that the situation was beyond us. You may even be experiencing that right now, whether it's a broken relationship with a loved one, the loss of a business, the pain of disease, or some other personal disaster. In those dark and stressful moments, anxiety, excessive worry, a sense of failure, and intense pain eliminate our confidence, hope, and joy with no apparent answers or quick solutions in sight.

As we saw in the previous chapter, one of the seven final lessons that Jesus imparted to us from his cross was that the cross disciple will always face some degree of suffering while seeking to obediently carry out the Father's will and more perfectly follow his way. Just as Jesus endured great physical, emotional, and spiritual pain as he agonized on his cross for our greater good and salvation, so too we must endure suffering as we carry out our own cross missions from him for his greater glory. But how exactly are we supposed to approach such agonizing moments, *especially when we feel like we can barely hang in there*?

In this chapter, I'll examine what Jesus hanging upon his cross can teach us about enduring and even embracing the suffering we experience as we "hang there" on our own crosses. Today we live in a world that thinks there's always an answer to every problem, a way to escape every sort of suffering. And if you can't solve it or escape it, then you just give up! But the truth is that some problems have no answers or ways to escape them—*you just have to endure them*. To overcome our agony in such dark moments, our one and only option as cross disciples of Jesus is to *hang there upon our cross and suffer just like Christ did*. After first looking a bit closer at our experience of suffering in this fallen world, we'll explore how Jesus's crucifixion radically reshapes

> **But the truth is that some problems have no answers or ways to escape them—*you just have to endure them*.**

how we, as his cross disciples, should think about "hanging in there" on our crosses and understand the role of suffering in our cross-carrying missions.

UNDERSTANDING OUR EXPERIENCE OF SUFFERING

About fifteen or twenty years into my ministry at University Baptist Church, I was told one Sunday by a church member, "Pastor, do you realize that almost half of your sermons are about suffering?" Good night, I couldn't believe it when I first heard that! But looking back, it makes sense that suffering would be such a common topic in my sermons. Our battles, trials, and struggles with suffering are a part of our daily lives, sometimes even more frequently than we realize.

When I was younger, I used to think that suffering was unnecessary, that it only happened to the foolish or to those who didn't have enough faith. As I grew up, I began to believe that although suffering may be a universal reality, I could avoid it if I was just smarter than everyone else. Later in life, my point of view changed again and I believed that while all of us experience some suffering, it could be managed. All I needed to do was just control it, defuse it, and minimize its effect on my life. But eventually I came to realize that suffering is ultimately inevitable—no matter what any of us do, we will all experience suffering in our lives. I finally realized the answer.

We all experience suffering in our lives because our world is fallen due to what Adam and Eve did in the Garden of Eden, an event we'll talk about again later in this book. We live in a broken world full of warfare and rebellion, natural disaster and atrocity, disease and the deceit of rampant demonic influence. Suffering is inevitable given those conditions. None of us can escape it on this earth. All that being said, we can still learn something from suffering and even find blessings in its brokenness with the Holy Spirit enabling us to think above it.

To start, it is through suffering that we discover for ourselves not only the truth that our world is fallen but also the depths of Christ's love for us in that brokenness. In fact, it is out of our experiences with suffering that we first seek out salvation, rebirth, and reconciliation through Christ. This means suffering should not be viewed simply as something to be avoided, managed, or despaired of. Rather, suffering can be a positive *invitation* for one to find salvation and respond to Christ's sacrificial love. Most times, it is in the face of suffering that we really begin to recognize his grace and truth, and it is in those moments of spiritual pain that we finally find ourselves needing to come to God. As one famous writer once said, "Thank God for the pain that brought Christ to my bedside."

But suffering is not just an invitation to salvation. As we'll continue to see in the chapters to follow, suffering is also a key part of what it means to live as a cross disciple. Sometimes our mission as cross disciples will involve suffering as we obediently follow his will. In those moments, the cross disciple will be called to *embrace* suffering as an *opportunity* placed before him or her by God. This type of suffering is different than the circumstantial suffering that comes from living in a broken world. Instead, this is the type of suffering that comes from joining with Christ in his cross-carrying and cross-hanging mission.

The distinction between the circumstantial suffering that we experience living in a fallen world and the suffering embraced by the cross disciple can be illustrated in the disastrous earthquake and tsunami that occurred in Japan in 2011. This natural disaster caused great *circumstantial suffering* for those who lived through it. But the tsunami also offered Christians the opportunity to join in the *cross-carrying suffering* of Christ by responding to the crisis through prayer, personal donations, and the work of missionaries who tirelessly cared for the survivors, even at the risk of their own lives. In this scenario, the suffering caused by the disaster itself is different than the suffering embraced by cross disciples in order to extend the love of the Messiah to the victims. Such moments of circumstantial suffering are opportunities for Christians to take up their cross, follow Christ, and, in the words of Paul, participate in Christ's sufferings and become like him in his death (Phil. 3:10).

As we can see, suffering is not only an inevitable experience that all humans encounter every day of their lives but also a significant part of what it means to be a cross disciple. Certainly, the cross disciple will face the same painful circumstances that all humans face on this fallen earth. But the cross disciple must also be ready to face the suffering that comes from obeying the Messiah's call. In the words of Paul, "it has been granted to you on behalf of Christ not only to believe in him, but also to suffer for him" (Phil. 1:29). But what does it mean to participate in Christ's sufferings? How should we, as cross disciples, seek to endure and even embrace suffering in our lives?

Learning How to Hang in There

As mentioned earlier in this book, the crucifixion of Jesus Christ represents the greatest scene in God's drama of redemption. Through his agonizing death, Jesus brought salvation and reconciliation to fallen humanity. But the significance of his cross does not end there. His cross also serves as an example—the ultimate symbol—that demonstrates how each of us should take up, carry, hang upon, and endure our own cross.

We can learn a lot about enduring suffering and hanging upon our own crosses by closely observing the fortitude Jesus had as he suffered upon the cross. As we saw in chapter 1, there has never been a type of death invented by humanity more horrible, brutal, painful, or agonizing than crucifixion. And that was the test that God chose for his Son. For six hours, Jesus endured extreme torture and humiliation while hanging upon his cross. God the Father could have easily had Jesus die a quick and nearly painless death by a spear to the heart or an axe to the neck. But instead, Jesus endured the suffering of his crucifixion. He hung upon his cross until God's purposes were fulfilled in his life.

There are several lessons that we can learn about how we should approach the suffering we encounter on our cross missions by looking at how Christ hung upon his cross. We must remember that hanging upon each of our crosses is our duty as cross disciples; that when we become absorbed in our cross-hanging missions, we mysteriously join with Christ's own crucifixion and become transformed by his life-giving spirit; and that although our cross-hanging mission will be difficult, there is also joy, comfort, and freedom in it.

Hanging upon Our Cross Is Our Duty

The first lesson we learn from Jesus about hanging upon our cross is that we must see suffering as part of our *duty* as cross disciples. Jesus didn't go to his cross to be rescued or to escape suffering. He went to the cross knowing that he would suffer agonizing pain because that was his duty. It was necessary in the mind of the Father.

We can see this in Jesus's prayer in the Garden of Gethsemane. The night before His crucifixion, Jesus was overcome with sorrow. While in Gethsemane, he fell facedown upon the ground and prayed: "My Father, if it is not possible for this cup to be taken away unless I drink it, may your will be done" (Matt. 26:42). When Jesus said to his Father, "your will be done," *he conformed his needs to his Father's command*. Jesus didn't go to the cross because he thought it was going to be easy; he knew that it wasn't going to feel good. It was going to be agony! For Jesus, his cross was the cup from which he had to drink to complete the Father's will for all humanity, and so he did just that.

Many years ago, I had the opportunity to speak with Brigadier General Paul Tibbets, who was the pilot-commander of the Enola Gay, the B-29 aircraft that dropped the first atomic bomb on Hiroshima on August 6, 1945. During our short conversation, I asked General Tibbets if he had many spiritual experiences leading up to the mission or afterward. He looked right at me, noting my chaplain's cross on my air force uniform, and said kindly but sternly, "My mind was fixed on one thing only . . . doing my duty."

I learned a great lesson in this brief exchange. Just as General Tibbets had one duty that his mind was solely fixed upon, so too our Messiah Jesus had one singular duty: to place his body upon the cross. Being a true Christian is a battle. And in this battle, our first and most important duty as cross disciples is to take up our cross and follow Jesus. Focusing on and doing this specific duty is always the answer, even if it demands great risk, suffering, or sacrificial obedience. But we cannot bear our cross and obediently fulfill our duty unless we do as Jesus did and pledge to the Father "your will be done." This means giving up our needs and desires to follow the will and command of God.

As cross disciples, we must make the big decision to pursue the cross as opposed to chasing after our own earthly wants. The world is full of *need-chasers*. What the church needs here and now are *cross-seekers*, those who want to find the cross in their lives, take up the cup the Father wills for them, and drink from it to his glory. We must allow our cross-bearing and cross-hanging mission to dominate our *attitudes* and determine our *actions*.

However, before we can fulfill our cross-hanging duty, we must first discern the cross we are called to hang upon. We must humbly, continually, regularly, and prayerfully ask him about the specifics of the cross-hanging mission he assigns us to embrace. We must each ask how we are supposed to suffer for him and where we are supposed to encounter our cross. We must each ask him what our cross will look like and when we must pick it up and suffer upon it. We must each ask him what our cross demands of us and how long we must carry and hang upon it. Finally, we must ask him whether this is really the cross he wants us to hang upon or if this suffering is simply from our own foolishness or some demonic deception.

I don't know what specific cross you are called to carry in your life right now; every single one of us has a different cross we are called to hang upon, a different cup we are called to drink from at any given time. (Man, I can barely understand my own cross sometimes!) But I promise you that if you want to know where the cross is in your life, God will show it to you.

The cross-hanging experiences that cross disciples encounter in life do not come at random. Each cross that we are meant to bear has been assigned to us by Christ! The cross that each of us is called to carry and hang upon will always come as a result of following in his steps as we strive to obey his voice. In fact, our own redemption is made increasingly real to us when we are enduring our own cross actions for the Father's glory!

Hanging upon Our Cross is Transformative

According to Scripture, when we hang upon our cross just as Christ did, we don't stay the same. On the contrary, our cross-hanging experience will *transform* who we are. Take, for instance, the words of the apostle Paul:

> I have been crucified with Christ and I no longer live, but Christ lives in me. The life I now live in the body, I live by faith in the Son of God, who loved me and gave himself for me. (Gal. 2:20)

For Paul, when we take up and suffer upon our cross, our old self that dominates and controls our lives is spiritually crucified and the life-giving spirit of Christ comes to take charge within us. In other words, when we embrace our cross-hanging mission, Christ himself will transform who we are from within.

It is important to note that what Paul says here is more than a metaphor or figure of speech—it is a deep and mysterious divine process. In the Father's eyes, we really died when Jesus did, and this changes everything about who we are and what happens when we choose to embrace our own cross suffering. When each of us chooses to suffer on our own cross, we become absorbed into the drama of redemption, and we begin to understand the mystery of Christ's cross as well as his divine love, grace, and righteousness. We really begin to incarnate the crucifixion and resurrection reality of Jesus in our own lives! This is a great miracle that is far too staggering for us to appreciate fully.

Of course, this doesn't mean that our old sinful nature stops trying to constantly attack us. It is impossible to follow the Savior perfectly, even if it is our deepest yearning! As Paul observes in Romans 7:14–25, our sinful natures will always be there to prevent us from doing what is good. No Christian has ever followed the Lord perfectly on this fallen earth populated by sin-diseased people. However, when we become crucified with Christ, the Savior's crucifixion activates to redeem our sinful natures and empowers us to take up and hang upon our cross adequately, sufficiently, competently, satisfactorily, and sometimes even abundantly! It is when we seek out, accept, and hang upon our cross that Christ steadily uplifts and transforms us so that we can please God and help others! In this way, our somewhat rare crucifixions can bring greater life to the world, just as the Savior's own hanging brought the Father's promise to all humanity.

But in order for our cross-hanging missions to transform us, we cannot take up our cross only part of the time or only when we feel like doing so. In the words of Paul, being a cross disciple means we must be prepared to bear and suffer upon our cross each and every day (1 Cor. 15:31–34). This is what it means to not escape dying daily. In one of my favorite pieces of Scripture on this subject, Paul states even more explicitly what it means to hang upon one's cross every day:

> We always carry around in our body the death of Jesus, so that the life of Jesus may also be revealed in our body. For we who are alive are always being given over to death for Jesus' sake, so that his life may also be revealed in our mortal body. So then, death is at work in us, but life is at work in you. (2 Cor. 4:10–12)

Every day, we as cross disciples are called to repeat Jesus's crucifixion and death within our own bodies so that we may yield to his life-giving Spirit. We must allow our self-centered lives to die so that we may live in the Spirit. In doing so, we manifest the resurrection life and love of Jesus to the world around us. When we truly give our lives to follow him, we find ourselves constantly adopting his *cross attitude* so that our mortal flesh can be transformed to perform his *cross actions*. In other words, when we daily let Jesus's *cross death* work in us, we can bring his *cross life* to the world. Our cross attitudes and actions offer the Savior's transformative cross benefits to others!

The more radically we experience and learn the wisdom of spiritually hanging upon our cross, the more radically the cross will transform us and conform us to Christ's image. When we truly decide to take up our cross and hang upon it, our minds and hearts become more like those of Christ. But first, we must be willing to be daily transformed by the cross he gives us if we are to triumph as cross disciples!

Hanging upon Our Cross will be Difficult

Finally, we must each fully understand that the specific, cross-hanging duty the Lord may assign us—the cup he might call us to drink from, the portion he might call us to bear, the life he might call us to live—will likely not be a quick or easily won battle. When our Master hung upon his cross, he experienced the most painful form of death ever invented on the face of this earth. For six hours, he endured incredible anguish and humiliation as he earnestly waited for the Father's hand to deliver him.

If, as Paul says, we are to be "crucified with Christ," then we are being called to share in an exhausting and excruciating experience, not a fast or easy one. It goes without saying that none of us like to suffer. Most of us can stand suffering if it's over quickly or we can find an explanation for it. But, as I said at the beginning of the chapter, some types of suffering don't just go away or have a good solution. During such suffering, many of us have said something like, "How much longer must I endure this?" or "How much can I take of this?" or "This is too much." We all have our unique ways of complaining when times get tough! Complaining is just one of many ways in which people respond to such agonizing situations. Some allow themselves to become defeated or embittered by their issues. Others deny that such problems even exist and choose to live in their own fantasy. Still others try to seek out instant pleasure or gratification to numb the pain.

Yet, when we look at the crucifixion, we find that the Lord Jesus didn't do any of these things. For six hours he did nothing but hang there. In these agonizing moments of life, we too need to follow Jesus's example and just hang there. This means enduring the anguish and difficulties we've been assigned on our cross mission without chasing after the things of the flesh, seeking some kind of earthly idol, or allowing ourselves to be consumed by despair or bitterness. Instead, it means gratefully accepting God's plan and totally submitting ourselves to the Father's will, just like Jesus did. But this is rarely easy. It's why so many Christians can show up on Sunday but don't want any part of their cross-hanging mission the rest of the week! Indeed, the cross you and I have been assigned may demand everything from us. The transformative, mysterious experience of hanging upon our cross is a process that is often extremely exhausting and excruciating before it becomes enlightening and exalting!

The cross realities assigned to us by the Master may certainly make things get far worse before they become better. Yet, when we endure and embrace struggles as Christ did with endurance and fortitude, it is then that we also encounter joy, comfort, and freedom. As the book of Hebrews states: "For the joy set before him [Jesus] endured the cross, scorning its shame, and sat down at the right hand of the throne of God" (Heb. 12:2b). Talk about a contrast! There can be joy where we're hanging there as part of our cross mission—joy and pain can exist at the same time when we are suffering for him! When we authentically seek, find, and embrace God's plan, our suffering can give us joy knowing that we are playing our part in God's drama of redemption. In my own life, I have experienced this exact thing—I go regularly from agony to ecstasy as I carry the cross and drink from the cup he has assigned

> Yet, when we endure and embrace struggles as Christ did with endurance and fortitude, it is then that we also encounter joy, comfort, and freedom.

me! The scorning of shame that Jesus achieved upon the cross is loaded with redemptive meaning for the cross disciple.

Fortunately, we may take comfort knowing that we do not suffer our cross alone. If we truly belong to the Lord, he will be with us in power as we carry our specific cross at the times he impresses us to hang with him! No matter the pressure, perplexity, and pain of our cross, no matter its cost or the "hang time" we must endure, we can take comfort knowing that the Lord knows what he is doing with us and will complete his mission through us. Remember, while we may share in Christ's sufferings, we also share in his life-giving spirit that transforms us.

Finally, when we authentically hang upon our cross, we discover new freedom from the fallen world around us. As Paul writes, "May I never boast except in the cross of our Lord Jesus Christ, through which the world has been crucified to me, and I to the world" (Gal. 6:14). When we partake in Christ's crucifixion by hanging upon our own crosses, the world also becomes crucified to us, freeing us from its pointless pursuits. We become dead to the world, no longer dominated by its empty idols and illusions. Again, this doesn't mean that we've overcome our old sinful natures completely. Rather, when we daily embrace, experience, and understand our part as cross-hanging disciples, Christ empowers us to see the delusional sins of the world as secondary, trivial, or irrelevant. In this manner, our cross-hanging mission radically changes how we encounter our fallen world and the suffering we experience.

To LEARN HOW TO HANG on our cross, just as the Savior did upon his, is not an optional choice but an inescapable reality in order to discover eternal life as a disciple of Jesus. *Hanging is a necessity before we can triumph.* We must daily seek to recognize the cross Christ calls us to hang upon and the cup the Father calls us to drink from. We must incarnate his cross mission in our lives by taking up the cross he has assigned us in our minds and hearts and then follow this task by adopting Christ-centered thoughts, words, and actions. We must be willing to carry the real-world responsibility of our cross, to endure whatever it might demand, and continually yield to Messiah's voice as he speaks and leads us to what's next. It is only then that we can authentically proclaim what I believe is the greatest, most significant, and most magnificent statement that could ever be spoken on this earth: "Father, into your hands I commit my spirit" (Luke 23:46).

Most Christians don't seem to prioritize identifying and distinguishing the cross-hanging duty they have been assigned and the suffering that such a mission brings with it, much less seek to embrace it! But the truth is that it is only when we hang upon the cross assigned to us by the Father that we truly discover what it means to follow Jesus and learn his joy in overcoming suffering. This won't be easy. Hanging upon your cross may leave you feeling helpless and hurt, hapless and hopeless, hampered and harassed, harried and hurried. But when we each suffer upon the cross we have been assigned, God will transform us into triumphant cross disciples who can discover joy, comfort, and freedom even in the face of suffering.

Of course, before we can even begin this task, we must first prayerfully ask Jesus to guide our cross attitudes and actions despite our dense, selfish, and foolish minds. We must ask the Messiah to allow his perceptions, purpose, power, and peace to use us for his profit and pleasure. Above all, however, we must cry out for Christ to teach us what it really means to deny ourselves, take up our cross daily, and follow him, and, in the process, carry around in our bodies his death so that we may bring life to others.

QUESTIONS FOR REFLECTION

1) What are some of the different ways people approach those "hang in there" moments in life? What are some of the problems with these methods of dealing with suffering?

2) In what way(s) can suffering be a positive thing? Can you think of a time when a moment of suffering made a positive impact on your faith?

3) What were the three main lessons concerning suffering covered in this chapter? How can we practically apply these lessons to our personal encounters with suffering in our cross-carrying journeys?

4) What do you think it means to help others through their suffering as cross disciples? Give a couple of practical examples of what this might look like.

CHAPTER 4

The Stages of Cross Discipleship

ONCE SOMEONE BECOMES A CHRIST follower, he or she encounters a new challenging question: What do we do now? Becoming a cross-carrying disciple and playing our small part in God's drama of redemption is a long, steady process just like any other great growth experience.

Over the years, I have developed a framework that has proved incredibly helpful in understanding the different stages on the cross-carrying path of the Christian life. Known as the U-A-O-Z Life model, this framework follows the upward arc of a person's development from an unbeliever to a saved child, then a maturing believer, and finally a veteran father or mother of the faith. The U-A-O-Z Life model gives us a basis for understanding how we, as Christ-followers, grow and become more effective, active, and pleasing to God in our roles as cross disciples.

In this chapter, we will explore the four stages of the U-A-O-Z Life model and how each one relates to our cross discipleship. We can briefly define the stages as follows:

U-Life: The *unbeliever* hungers for meaning, significance, and a deeper life. The "best" they can do is to strive to love as unconditionally as possible. They experience the suffering of this world but don't understand it. *They long for real life.* Unfortunately, they are still blind to what that real life really is.

A-Life: The *beginner believer* embraces salvation, healing, and wholeness in Christ. They experience a taste of the Messiah's love through faith in the redemption and invitation of the cross. *They come to eternal life.* For them, Jesus is real.

O-Life: The *maturing believer* continuously develops a cross discipleship lifestyle. They increasingly recognize that their human purpose is to possess and express the Messiah's love throughout their world by taking up their cross. *They learn eternal life.* For them, Jesus is faithful.

Z-Life: The *veteran believer* finds joy in living as a warrior of their Messiah's love. They embody and exude the Messiah's love to others by comprehending and following the Savior's cross pattern of incarnation, crucifixion, resurrection, and exaltation while walking the earth. *They live eternal life.* For them, Jesus is splendor.

These four stages should not be read too literally or mechanically. As humans made in his image, we may participate in all four levels throughout our lives, no matter what our primary hope and current level of belief might be. All cross disciples remain an experiential mix of our old creation in Adam and our new creation in Christ. As a result, biblical growth is not a static position that one permanently holds but a *dynamic reaction* to every moment-by-moment circumstance in our lives. This means one may experience many great leaps forward and many setbacks in the process: An unbeliever might see the salvation vision of the newborn Christian; a believer in the Z-Life stage might slip and make an immature A-Life stage mistake; an O-Life believer might fear the cross involved in growing into the Z-Life stage.

> **Biblical growth is not a static position that one permanently holds but a *dynamic reaction* to every moment-by-moment circumstance in our lives.**

All of us will grow differently according to our personal gifts, struggles, and sacrifices as well as the Lord's timing. Indeed, each experience at every stage of cross-carrying offers us the opportunity to change. And, as we all know from such experiences, Christian growth is not maintained without effort! Such growth is only possible and sustainable by steadily depending upon Jesus and the Holy Spirit who was sent to teach, guide, and protect us. The key here is *yielding* to the Godhead who loves you and is speaking to you all the time through your experience of creation, your study of the Scriptures, and your listening to the Holy Spirit. This is God's voice of *truth*. Every stage of cross discipleship will involve yielding ever more to God's truth.

1 John 2:12–14 and the Stages of Cross Discipleship

The stages of the Christian life featured in the U-A-O-Z Life model are based upon the great truth expressed in 1 John 2. Here the beloved disciple, the apostle John, addresses his letter to three primary groups of disciples:

> I am writing to you, *dear children,*
> because your sins have been forgiven on account of his name.
> I am writing to you, *fathers,*
> because you know him who is from the beginning.
> I am writing to you, *young men,*
> because you have overcome the evil one.
> I write to you, *dear children,*
> because you know the Father.
> I write to you, *fathers,*
> because you know him who is from the beginning.
> I write to you, *young men,*
> because you are strong,
> and the word of God lives in you,
> and you have overcome the evil one. (1 John 2:12–14, emphasis added)

I believe that this division was no accident; the apostle must have been led by the Spirit to divide the disciples into these three groups. His insights are specific and match how we experience reality as children, young adults, and mature parents.

When addressing the *children*, John characterizes their lives in two ways: They have come to know their heavenly Father, and they have been forgiven of all their sins because of his love. Are these not the first two things all happy and healthy children must learn? Little ones must know who loves them and that they are unconditionally accepted. My infant great-granddaughter has started to reveal her will by knowing who her momma is and wanting the comfort of her love. She can't define love, but she knows, needs, and wants it! Children with godly parents or guardians know that *they are loved* and that *they are secure*!

Next, John says three things to the *young men*: They are learning how to overcome the evil one, they are growing in spiritual strength, and the Word of God is alive to them as they encounter life. We can speak of these young men (and women) as spiritual warriors who are learning how to defend the church, battle for righteousness, and embrace the cross as their strength. This means that these growing warriors of the cross must be *strong, powerful, and energetic*; they must allow *the Word of God to be vital in their minds, hearts, and ambitions*; and they must *consistently defeat Satan's attacks on their lives*!

Finally, the apostle addresses the *fathers* (and mothers), the combat veterans of the cross. The apostle has only one thing to say to them: Their authority and assurance are complete because they have known "him who is from the beginning." Note that John doesn't say that these spiritual veterans "know *all things* from the beginning" but that they "know *him* who is from the beginning." In fact, they have learned the *one thing necessary* according to the Lord Jesus (Luke 10:41–42). To know and love him always trumps responding to and appreciating whatever he has done, might do, or intends to do! Therefore, these fathers and mothers are leaders of the faith who need and desire only one thing: *to know him and to make his magnificence and wonder known to others.*

These three levels of Christian discipleship given to us in 1 John 2 provide a model for understanding the different stages of cross discipleship that we may grow into and experience throughout our lives. We will now explore in more detail each of these three stages as well as the life of the unbeliever.

The Unbeliever (U-Life): Hungering for More

The unbeliever's life—known in the U-A-O-Z Life model as the U-Life—is the inescapable, unfruitful, and temporary existence of those who are slaves to themselves. To use the words of Jesus found in Mark 8:34–38, the unbeliever's life is driven by the *purposeless passions* of world-gaining love, such that they may "gain the world, yet forfeit their soul." Living the U-Life is to embrace the illusionary path of our fallen world into despair (1 John 2:15–17).

All human beings are destined to live in the U-Life stage until they seek, find, and receive Jesus as their personal Savior and sovereign Deliverer. According to our Lord, relatively few appear to enter this small and narrow gate that leads to life (Matt. 7:13–14). Unbelievers need to receive the Father's good news of grace and truth as well as yield themselves to the Savior's discipleship of the cross. Here it is important to define what we mean by *grace* and *truth*. *Grace* can be defined as God's initiative of love on our behalf, whereas *truth* is his standard of reality that we cannot escape. Jesus in his flesh was full of both grace and truth (John 1:14–18).

Like all human beings, those in the U-Life stage have been created in the image of our triune God (Gen. 1:27). However, unlike those who have progressed further in the U-A-O-Z Life arc, those living in the U-Life stage miss the power and energy of cross reality and, in the words of Paul, they think that "the message of the cross is foolishness" (1 Cor. 1:18). They are therefore blind to Jesus Christ and perceive reality only partially and ineffectively. While unbelievers can acknowledge that they are alive in creation, they cannot perceive the Savior God behind creation (Rom. 1:20). Despite this, the Good Shepherd has compassion on his sheep, including those who are currently lost, and will bless or use them in fulfilling his purposes. The Good Shepherd has compassion on everyone, and he still wants all unbelievers to come to repentance, reject sin, and accept him (Mark 6:34; 2 Pet. 3:9).

Unbelievers can experience growth and progress toward God's grace and truth, even though they live in only a *partial world* without knowledge of the power of our saving Lord. At first, an unbeliever may only live for himself or herself. They exalt their own life and prioritize their own successes. They strive to dominate the culture and world around them. They proclaim "For me to live is *me*!" and see themselves as "playing god" with their gifts and time, as there is nothing and no one else to live for.

Eventually, however, those living in the U-Life stage encounter reality as unsatisfactory, unawake, and unsaved. In addition to being blind to or ignorant of the potential joy of the Messiah and his redemption, they still experience the grief of life's inevitable battles. Enduring the struggles of life without the security and riches promised by our loving Creator, who desires that these sheep that he *created* become his sheep by *recreation*, they realize that they are unable to escape these earthly depressions and destruction.

Those unbelievers who hunger for more than their current existence may seek out greater significance, meaning, or some sort of truth. They'll look for something more than themselves and declare "For me to live is *more than just me*!" Once awakened, the unbeliever may start to consider God and his mystery as much as they are able to. But the best they can do is to strive to love as unconditionally as they can. Therefore, we must continuously seek to influence their vision of and attraction to Messiah Jesus as we live out our own cross discipleship.

If one is to move beyond the U-Life and find ultimate meaning, significance, and joy, he or she must discover and receive the lavish, extravagant gift that the Father offers us in Christ Jesus. Only fools place God's gift anywhere but first place in their lives. Those who receive this gift and yield to the Messiah are led to live eagerly, positively, and progressively through the stages of the Christian life. The person who has made John 1:12 the foundation of their lives is secure and satisfied forever: "Yet to all who did receive him, to those who believed in his name, he gave the right to become children of God."

THE BEGINNER BELIEVER (A-LIFE):
PLAYING AT CARRYING OUR CROSS

In Revelation 1:8, the Lord Jesus says he is the *alpha* (A) and the *omega* (Ω), which are the first and last letters of the Greek alphabet. It's like saying "from A to Z." In other words, "I am the total package from beginning to end!" Christ-followers move from A to Z as they progress through the Christian life. We start as beginner believers exploring the first letters (i.e., the ABCs) of our faith (hence the term *A-Life*) before becoming more mature believers and learning the middle and final letters of the alphabet.

Whereas all human beings have been created in the image of God, as noted above, the beginner believer has "put on the new self, which is being renewed in knowledge in the image of its Creator" (Col. 3:10). The A-Life follower has heard the call to come and is discovering the people of God, having been accepted into the family of redemption through his or her second birth. The beginner believer is thus a baby believer. In the words of 1 John 2:12–14, they are the newborn *children* of the family of faith.

The greatest gain any human being can ever experience is salvation. It is the starting point for all believers. Our Lord himself shows us how to come to salvation in his encounter with Nicodemus in John 3. Here are a few important verses to remind us of the wonder and mystery of salvation.

> Now there was a Pharisee, a man named Nicodemus who was a member of the Jewish ruling council. He came to Jesus at night and said, "Rabbi, we know that you are a teacher who has come from God. For no one

69

could perform the signs you are doing if God were not with him."

Jesus replied, "Very truly I tell you, no one can see the kingdom of God unless they are born again."

"How can someone be born when they are old?" Nicodemus asked. "Surely they cannot enter a second time into their mother's womb to be born!"

Jesus answered, "Very truly I tell you, no one can enter the kingdom of God unless they are born of water and the Spirit. Flesh gives birth to flesh, but the Spirit gives birth to spirit. You should not be surprised at my saying, 'You must be born again.' The wind blows wherever it pleases. You hear its sound, but you cannot tell where it comes from or where it is going. So it is with everyone born of the Spirit."

"How can this be?" Nicodemus asked. . . .

"For God so loved the world that he gave his one and only Son, that whoever believes in him shall not perish but have eternal life. For God did not send his Son into the world to condemn the world, but to save the world through him." (John 3:1–9, 16–17)

This is the starting point for all believers. We all enter the faith as born-again newborns growing into babies and then—if we are growing as we should—into children. We all start as A-Life believers, as recruits in the army of the Lord who have taken our seats in God's drama of redemption in the hopes of understanding Jesus's great sacrificial act and its continuous significance in our lives.

The greatest gains of the A-Life are finding salvation and beginning to grow out of the worldly way of being, thinking, and doing while starting to repeat the life of Jesus Christ. While the unbeliever in the U-Life stage grows by learning to hunger for something more, the A-Life believer grows by learning the truth of Messiah Jesus and the hope that is in him. The A-Life believer's priority is to *find their Christ life*. These baby believers enter a period of meaningful discovery where they perceive the small picture and their identity as a new creation (2 Cor. 5:17). Just as babies are accepted unconditionally by loving parents, so too these spiritual children are totally loved and accepted by their Father in heaven.

> The A-Life believer's priority is to *find their Christ life.*

They live in the security and wholeness of the truth that they are perfect in the sight of Christ (Heb. 10:14). As born-again, believing children, they learn the ABCs of the cross. They desire the milk of the Word as newborns who have tasted the Lord's goodness (1 Pet. 2:2–3). These beginner believers are untested in heavy battle. They rejoice most in *receiving* from God.

During this stage, A-Life followers must also come to experience, comprehend, and accept two basic realities. First, they must taste the beginnings of spiritual freedom and abundant life (John 3:1–8). They must discover the empowering reality of God's love by meeting him personally and knowing that their sins are all forgiven. Second, they must also taste the wonder of the Lord's salvation intentions and expectations (1 Cor. 2:6–10). As they give their time to know Christ, these beginner believers, to paraphrase the words of Paul, must strive to become fully aware of his power, mind, suffering, cross, and resurrection in the *now* (Phil. 3:10–11). A-Life believers live to follow Christ so that they may save themselves for him. The beginner believer declares, in contrast to the unbeliever, "For me to live is *Christ*!"

As spiritual children, A-Life believers *play at carrying their cross*, as children are supposed to do. To say they "play" at carrying their cross should not be read as a frivolous activity. When one is a child, play is the first step in learning how to do many serious things. It is only when our play does not advance to practice that problems may arise. Indeed, the beginner believer must not remain a spiritual child their entire life. In the words of Paul, they must "no longer be infants" (Eph. 4:14). The A-Life follower possesses knowledge of the Lord Jesus, but this knowledge is inadequate if they are to grow up and become increasingly conformed to the persuasive and inviting image of the likeness of Christ Jesus. Here, I think of Paul's rebuke in 1 Corinthians 3:1–3a:

> Brothers and sisters, I could not address you as people who live by the Spirit but as people who are still worldly—mere infants in Christ. I gave you milk, not solid food, for you were not yet ready for it. Indeed, you are still not ready. You are still worldly.

These baby believers were dear to the great apostle, and he desired that they might gain more of Christ rather than stall their growth by worldly bickering. Unfortunately, many in our churches today suffer from the same childish lack of growth Paul saw among his friends in Corinth. To quote the gospel song "The Highway to Heaven," they know they have "a heaven to gain and a hell to shun," but they have yet to grasp how many treasures they have to gain by fully turning themselves from the worldly to walk by the Spirit (Gal. 5:16–18).

THE MATURING BELIEVER (O-LIFE): LEARNING TO CARRY THE CROSS

If A-Life believers are those who are learning the basic ABCs of God's love and forgiveness, then those more mature believers are those who have advanced to confronting the deeper realities and challenges of the fall. We call these believers O-Life disciples because they are learning the middle letters (that is, the MNOPs) of the Christian life. Those living in the O-Life stage are the *young warriors* mentioned in 1 John 2:12–14. These maturing disciples have entered an engaging level of growth where they are *learning* their faith and *practicing* cross discipleship. They have begun to give their efforts to serving Christ in the power of the Holy Spirit.

Unlike the A-Life believers who perceive only the small picture and their status as a *new creation*, O-Life disciples perceive the big picture and their calling to *be creative* and do great things for the Father and for others (John 14:11–14). They have moved from a period of *meaningful discovery* to a stage where they are becoming a *maturing sacrifice*. They have not only started to attend the theater of God and closely contemplate Jesus's cross, but they have also begun to authentically seek out their own part in his redemptive drama. Like the worthy servants in Jesus's parable of the talents (Matt. 25:14–30), maturing believers seek to be good stewards of the gifts that have been entrusted to them.

Compared to the spiritual children of the A-Life, these maturing warriors know the difference between milk and solid food, and they recognize that constant training is necessary to continually taste the wonder of righteousness and to distinguish between good and evil (Heb. 5:11–14). O-Life disciples know they must advance to the cross issues of the Christian experience (the MNOPs) if they are to develop a life of prevailing impact for the Savior's mission. In the process, these maturing warriors gain different degrees of experience and overcome various challenges as they engage in spiritual combat. They acquire wisdom and power from the Scriptures, overcome satanic deception, and grow stronger in the mature matters of what Christ's cross can and should mean to their lives (1 John 2:12–14). In the process, they begin to taste the beginnings of sanctification in their cross life. These O-Life believers experience the sanctifying promises of the Lord as he makes them holy and opens their eyes to his perfection and their own (Heb. 10:14). As a result, they rejoice most in *achieving* for God as they explore the depths of his love, hungering for more of the Father and his mission.

Those disciples in the O-Life stage live not only to save themselves for Christ but *to be a success for him*. They have not only found life in Christ but allow their lives to be dominated by Christ. Whereas the newborn recruit in the A-Life stage may want to escape suffering, the O-Life warrior examines suffering as he or she counts the cost of ministry. O-Life disciples know that they must know the truth of the Word of God, overcome the evil in their lives, and remain strong.

The Veteran Believers (Z-Life):
Living the Cross-Carrying Life

Finally, we come to the veteran believers—the elders, the men and women who have been heavily tested in their faith. These disciples are the *fathers* (or elders) from 1 John 2:12–14. They are called Z-Life believers because they have learned even the very last letters of the Christian life, cross discipleship, and the spiritual battle (the XYZs).

Z-life disciples are combat veterans who have already experienced and been wounded in the type of heavy spiritual battle being fought by the O-Life warriors. Z-Life Christians are thus eager partners of righteousness and know well the reality of the cross. They are totally content *knowing* most deeply who he is, *yielding* to his words, and *possessing* his purpose and pleasure. They *taste* and *eat* Christ's body and blood daily (John 6:58–59) and have a high level of participation in the Savior's Messiah heart, vision, and passion (Phil. 3:7–18). They rejoice most in simply believing in God and demonstrating the grace of the Messiah by learning and manifesting his love.

These veteran disciples perceive not just the *big picture* but the *entire God-picture*. They not only know that they are a *new creation* in Christ (A-Life) and follow *their call to create* (O-Life), but they also find themselves *at one with their Creator* (John 17:20–24). Veteran disciples of the cross give their lives by striving to die upon their crosses for Christ and his sheep daily (John 10:14–18; 15:13). They are always sacrificing their lives for the one thing that matters. They are the disciples most experienced and intimate with the hidden yet revealed eternal purposes of the cross and the sanctification workings in their personal cross life. Z-Life believers have tested and are fully satisfied that the will of God alone brings us what is good, pleasing, and perfect. They possess a wise and mature hunger for the mysterious riches of Christ in us (Col. 1:24–29).

These spiritual fathers and mothers have begun to grasp *the deepest of the Lord's eternal intentions* (John 17:3). They know they exist to most fully live out the mind of Christ described in Philippians 2:5–11:

> In your relationships with one another, have the same mindset as Christ Jesus:
> Who, being in very nature God,
> did not consider equality with God something to be
> used to his own advantage;
> rather, he made himself nothing
> by taking the very nature of a servant,
> being made in human likeness.
> And being found in appearance as a man,
> he humbled himself
> by becoming obedient to death—
> even death on a cross!
> Therefore God exalted him to the highest place
> and gave him the name that is above every name,
> that at the name of Jesus every knee should bow,
> in heaven and on earth and under the earth,
> and every tongue acknowledge that Jesus Christ is Lord,
> to the glory of God the Father.

In this manner, the veteran disciples who have risen to the Z-Life envision the Father's creation, redemption, and perfection purposes for themselves! They embody the perfect pattern of Christ's life and his challenge for us to take up our cross and follow him. Their lives, perceptions, and ambitions revolve around his incarnation, crucifixion, resurrection, and exaltation.

The great reality for Z-Life disciples is their intimacy and oneness with the eternal God. As we saw earlier, the beloved disciple John had only one thing to say to the combat veterans of the cross addressed in 1 John 2:12–14—their authority and assurance is complete because they have known "him who is from the beginning." They *experience most fully* the Godhead's magnificent intent of love "from the beginning" because they "know him" most deeply. The veteran disciple's greatest treasure, wisdom, stature, contentment, and overcoming lies in *one thing alone*—to experientially know *him who is* from the beginning of all things! They are "in Christ," the One whom they have come to know as life eternal (2 Cor. 5:17; John 17:3).

When you have been around for eternity, as our heavenly Father has, a thousand years is a drop in the bucket, much less our eighty or ninety years of walking on this earth! Knowing, loving, and yielding to the eternal Father should be our primary answer to everything that challenges, confronts, and limits us. All of us are eager to know the mysteries of our lives. But the great *whys* of our existence—our struggles, suffering, shame, secrets, separations, sorrows, scars, satisfactions, and significance—constantly stun and stagger us. I confess that such questions used to consume me even as I fulfilled my normal duties and responsibilities in life. *Why is there evil in the world? Why does suffering exist? Why is this person so sad, helpless, and hopeless? Why does God love us in spite of our selfish, stupid, and sickening sin?* I could easily list a hundred more compelling and complex questions about God, earth, purpose, others, and myself!

But even if we had all the answers to all our questions, what would we profit? Besides, our finite capacity for knowledge could never begin to grasp the infinite glory and purpose of the eternal majesty beyond! The essence of our present earth life lies not in absorbing ourselves in our daily details or the great scientific questions of creation. No! Our most fervent ambition and priority passion should be: (1) to know personally his love, (2) to worship the immeasurableness of his life, (3) to accept every invitation to experience intimacy with our Creator, and (4) to live significantly for his will by yielding to every word the Holy Spirit tells us. Yet, most of us miss this main point time and time again! However, the fathers and mothers of the faith have learned that all they need is to know him who is from the beginning and to make his magnificence and wonder known to others as revealed by his Son, who brought us the fullness of grace and truth as our Lamb, Lion, and Lord.

All of us striving to live the Z-Life should therefore adopt the noble ambition so magnificently stated by the apostle Paul in Philippians 1:21, which I paraphrase as: *For me, to be fully alive is all about my identifying with, fathoming, and apprehending the mind and heart of Christ, and knowing my involvement with him is everything I hunger for! If I lose everything for his cause or even if I die, I will simply gain more of him and nothing in life surpasses that!* Have no doubt, my friend. This is a Z-level vision statement, a Z-level daily passion, and a Z-level act of trust. No goal or longing in life is more paramount, majestic, or illustrious for our significance and fulfillment! No aim or aspiration is more critical or urgent for our existence here and now! All else will be answered when the Lord knows we need it to fulfill his loving purpose for each of us as we dwell forever in his eternity.

IN OUR PROGRESSION FROM THE U-Life to the Z-Life, we must continually seek the mind of Christ so that we can increasingly see "the God picture" in every event, relationship, and situation and in all of our thoughts, actions, and responses. The cross disciple's constant goal in each stage of growth should be to expand his or her cross-centered learning while yielding to everything they can conceive concerning their Father in heaven. At every level of growth in the Christian life, we should seek to learn cross obedience.

As we seek to ascend the stages of cross discipleship, we must let the words of the Lord Jesus control our every movement as we obediently respond to his will. We must constantly reflect upon what Jesus says in Matthew 10:38–39:

> Whoever does not take up their cross and follow me
> is not worthy of me. Whoever finds their life will lose
> it, and whoever loses their life for my sake will find it.

At every stage of cross discipleship, we must consistently ask what it means to *take up our cross*. We must prayerfully consider what we each need to do to *follow him* moment by moment. We must seek out how our personal cross-carrying and cross-hanging missions can be *worthy* acts of worship for our Savior. Finally, we must truly understand what it looks like to *find and lose our lives for Jesus's sake.* It is when we strive to find the answers to these four questions that we experience growth in cross discipleship and come ever closer to hearing his words "Well done, good and faithful servant" (Matt. 25:23).

The Lord will deal with all of us at our varying maturity levels as he wills, when he wants, and as he knows is best. Wherever you are in this process—no matter how much you've grown or whatever part you're playing in his drama of redemption—listen intensely for his voice, fill and flood your mind with his Scriptures, and quickly yield to the guidance of his Spirit as best you sense it! Each one of us should earnestly and continuously study and pursue all the grace and truth we can about the Lord Jesus—from A to Z!

QUESTIONS FOR REFLECTION

1) Name the four stages of the U-A-O-Z Life model. What does each of the four letters stand for? How does 1 John 2:12–14 relate to the U-A-O-Z Life model?

2) Where does your life currently fit within the U-A-O-Z Life model? At what stage would you like to be at? What steps of growth do you need to take to get to that level?

3) What are the defining characteristics of the unbeliever's life (U-Life)? What are some practical ways that a cross disciple could help guide an unbeliever to the first stage of the Christian life?

4) How does the beginner believer's life (A-Life) differ from the veteran believer's life (Z-Life)? What are some spiritual practices that a newborn Christian could adopt to mature in their cross-discipleship journey?

CHAPTER 5

Experiencing Cross Discipleship

WHEN REFLECTING ON THE PROCESS described in the previous chapter of being personally transformed from the blind bondage of the U-Life to the blazing freedom of the Z-Life, I often think of the words of the apostle Paul from 1 Corinthians 13:11–13:

> When I was a child, I talked like a child, I thought like a child, I reasoned like a child. When I became a man, I put the ways of childhood behind me. For now we see only a reflection as in a mirror; then we shall see face to face. Now I know in part; then I shall know fully, even as I am fully known.
>
> And now these three remain: faith, hope and love. But the greatest of these is love.

Yes! When I was a child, I talked, thought, and acted like a child. And you did too. But, as Paul puts it, as we became grown adults, we put aside our childish ways. Sometimes when I look back at my younger self, I can't believe how unaware, dense, and blind I was to myself and to the world and the people around me! But now, in my highest maturity through Christ, I have more fully come to recognize that I must now pursue the combat veteran ways ahead of me and allow myself to be totally guided by the mind and heart of Christ, our heavenly commander who gives only perfect orders.

When a person encounters the Savior in a significant and impactful way and responds in humility and obedience, he or she enters a new life stage of discipleship. Think of Isaiah 6 and how Isaiah was already a prophet when he met God in the temple, but upon seeing the actual glory of God on his throne and being invited to join him in his work, Isaiah's life changed for the better. In the same way, when we become cross disciples, our life radically changes. The pinnacle of existence for the accomplished cross disciple is their extreme joy, secure contentment, and intense ambition to live every dimension and moment of life at the Z-Life level! Their primary ambition and passion should be to carry their Savior-assigned cross and not mess with human idols (Isa. 44:6–11; 1 John 5:21). In doing so, the believer participates in Jesus's divine nature, power, suffering, cross, cleansing, revelation, sanctification, and resurrection (Phil. 3:10–11). As we read in 2 Peter:

> His divine power has given us everything we need for a godly life through our knowledge of him who called us by his own glory and goodness. Through these he has given us his very great and precious promises, so that through them you may participate in the divine nature, having escaped the corruption in the world caused by evil distress. (2 Pet. 1:3–4)

All that is alive in our Messiah Lord becomes increasingly alive in the cross disciple!

In this chapter, we will explore five things one experiences as he or she walks after Jesus and moves from being an unbeliever to a Z-Life cross disciple who participates in the life of our Messiah Lord. We will see how experiencing *pain* leads one to seek the *gain* of salvation over the consequences of the fall; how this *gain* prompts the believer to recognize good over evil and *deign* the agony of their cross in order to reach down to others; and how this act of *deigning* empowers the believer to *reign* in this life by repeating the cross-carrying life of Jesus. Finally, it is through learning about *pain, gain, deign,* and *reign* that one moves from unbelief to spiritual childhood to their warrior adulthood and gradually to their veteran stage of cross discipleship. Here the cross disciple experiences the final and ultimate expression of what is possible in their earthly life—to *remain* in Jesus.

Pain

To become a worthy, cross-carrying servant of Messiah Jesus means we must first experience, comprehend, and endure the deception, destruction, dismay, dread, and death in our lives resulting from humanity's fall into sin in the Garden of Eden. *We must learn about pain.*

In his stupendous act of creation, the Godhead brought into being a world so complex and beautiful that the human mind continues to find it hard to grasp. The more we learn about it, the more we find to marvel over. But everything we see today is marred and diminished by the actions of humans long ago at the very beginning of human history (Rom. 8:19–23). According to Genesis 2–3, in the beginning the Creator put Adam and Eve in Eden, his garden of "delight" (in Hebrew, the word *eden* means "delight"). In the garden of delight, the Lord God prepared the *perfect place* for his *perfect couple* to live a *perfect life* totally pleasing to his *perfect will* in order to be in a perfect, purposeful relationship with their *perfect Creator*! Before the fall, Adam and Eve *worked* in the garden; they *worshiped* God; they *watched* over creation to make sure it was taken care of; they *walked* daily with him; and they *waited* for their Lord God's next action of revelation, purpose, sovereignty, and love. He even gave them one another to experience on a smaller scale that he is love!

Yet, tragedy came upon them. The Lord gave Adam and Eve a perfect paradise of desirous delight to live out their lives, to enjoy the excitement of his assigned work, to know the ecstasy of worshiping him, and to experience the thrill of walking with him and the expectant anticipation for his next act of love. But Satan, in the guise of a beautiful and wise snake, convinced them they were being cheated by their Creator, a delusion all humanity continues to fall for. Once convinced of this, they took their destiny out of their loving Creator's hands and naively followed the serpent's deceptions! Adam and Eve lost the possibility of the *delight of God* and were exiled from the Garden of Eden.

Adam and Eve were created to *work, worship, walk, watch,* and *wait* with total focus on God's perfect purpose and their fulfillment. But, because of their blindness, deception, rebellion, and sin, all humankind inherited an unsaved, diseased nature that is enslaved to the cravings of greedy flesh, the lusts of coveting eyes, and the prideful arrogance of irrelevant and self-centered living rather than the idyllic harmony the Creator intended. They forfeited their perfect, purposeful relationship with God!

The sad history of fleshly inhumanity and depravity began within the first generation. Amazing! The pervasive bane of sin and most of the pain we experience are a result of the broken obedience system imposed on creation by the fall of Adam and Eve. Radio personality Paul Harvey used to say that you can run but you can't hide from the problems of this world and the sad, bad things of human nature. Even a passing brush with current events makes this dreadfully clear. As every person who has ever lived can attest, this world and its brokenness bring physical, emotional, mental, and spiritual pain. Humanity is broken, diseased, and hopeless in its present condition. Our lives are under the curse of sin, and we suffer from the very act of living.

Earlier we observed how moving from the U-Life to the A-Life involves learning the implications of sin and the pain it brings. For the unbeliever to become a spiritual newborn, he or she must first come to know and experience the horror of the pain of the fall. They must realize they are unable to escape the struggles of life and the pressing problems of sin and therefore hunger for more than their current existence. There is only one solution. We must grow to hate sin as much as Jesus hates it! Only then can we protect ourselves and gain the advantage.

In addition to moving us toward salvation, understanding suffering also brings a cross disciple closer to the Savior. We saw in chapter 3 how suffering represents not only an inescapable reality of human existence but also a major part of what it means to become a cross disciple. Learning how to hang upon our cross and endure suffering as the Messiah did in his crucifixion is essential to our growth as cross-carrying followers of Jesus. And as we observed in the previous chapter, the different stages of our cross discipleship reflect differing attitudes toward suffering for the loving purposes of God. The A-Life child still wants to escape suffering, and the O-Life young adult counts suffering as part of the cost of ministry, but the Z-Life veteran has come to understand suffering enough to embrace it when the Lord places it before him or her.

We can witness firsthand what it means to understand and endure suffering in the book of Job. This biblical book recounts how Job, a wealthy and godly man, responded to catastrophic suffering of body, mind, and spirit. In one fell swoop, his livestock were taken from him, his children murdered, and Job became afflicted with painful sores. As Job himself put it, "Yet man is born to trouble as surely as sparks fly upward" (Job 5:7). However, after a long struggle with suffering, Job experiences a personal encounter with the Creator God himself. It is then that he reaches the conclusion of the matter, saying to God:

> "I know that you can do all things;
>   no purpose of yours can be thwarted. . . .
> My ears had heard of you but now my eyes have seen you.
> Therefore I despise myself and repent in dust and ashes." (Job 42:2, 5–6)

At the end of the book, Job discovers what it means to encounter God through suffering. And once this happens, Job is blessed by God with even more livestock and children than he lost through his previous suffering.

I believe we can discern a critical lesson here from Job. When the cross disciple encounters suffering, they must be able to learn how to address it as Job did: as an opportunity to learn in more depth about the Lord and his mysteries. Just as Job was eventually able to intimately encounter God and experience growth in the midst of his suffering, so too the cross disciple can encounter God and grow in their faith in the face of pain, loss, disappointment, and rejection.

As Paul writes in Romans 5:3–4: "Not only so, but we also glory in our sufferings, because we know that suffering produces perseverance; perseverance, character; and character, hope." Remember, this kind of suffering is done for a reason. It is not suffering for suffering's sake, but suffering embraced for our Lord Jesus's sake. If we take up this attitude, we will be able to embrace the honor of being "fools for Jesus's sake" and prove ourselves chosen to be given over to death for Jesus's sake (1 Cor. 4:5; 2 Cor. 4:10). We must learn pain to accept the reality of the human condition!

> Just as Job was eventually able to intimately encounter God and experience growth in the midst of his suffering, so too the cross disciple can encounter God and grow in their faith in the face of pain, loss, disappointment, and rejection.

Gain

To save ourselves from the *pain* of sin and find relief from its attacks, we must listen to the Spirit's redemptive call. Through accepting salvation and embracing an active faith, we *gain* the assurance and the vision that all of the Lord's gracious promises are eventually coming to us. Facing the bane of sin, we can be continuously comforted and without fear knowing that our Savior is sovereign, his endgame for his purposes is glorious, and his purposes include us! *We learn the gain of life.*

As just stated, the first step in finding the positive side of suffering in Christ must be salvation—our own rebirth and reconciliation to the God who sought us even when we turned from him to follow the ways of this world (Eph. 2:2). Humanity lost so much in the fall. Yet from the beginning, even before humanity first experienced death, a way to new life was revealed. In Genesis 3:15, God declares to Satan, the deceptive serpent, "I will put enmity between you and the woman, and between your offspring and hers; he will crush your head, and you will strike his heel."

In the very last book of the Scriptures, we witness the fulfillment of this promise. In Revelation 22, the apostle John describes the restoration of Eden, the garden of delight. A great river flows from the throne of God and the Lamb through the entire city alongside the Tree of Life. John reveals that "No longer will there be any curse. The throne of God and of the Lamb will be in the city, and his servants will serve him. . . . And they will reign for ever and ever" (Rev. 22:3, 5c). This is what we will gain in salvation!

The greatest gain a human being can ever experience is salvation. Our Lord shows us how to come to salvation in his encounter with Nicodemus in John 3, as we saw in chapter 4. This is the starting point for all believers. We all enter the faith as A-Life believers: newborn children and new recruits in the army of the Lord who have found their Christ life. Upon finding salvation, A-Life believers grow to love the Father's kingdom of love and perfection, just as Jesus did, and learn to carefully hear the Lord's voice and the gain of his call.

But salvation does not end there. An old adage puts it this way: We are saved (salvation), we are being saved (sanctification), and we will be saved (glorification). It is true that the greatest gain of the A-Life lies in finding salvation and starting to grow out of the worldly ways of being, thinking, and doing. But gain does not stop when an A-Life child becomes the O-Life maturing adult, or even when he or she becomes a Z-Life elder. Paul, one of the greatest Z-Life believers of all time, understood that gain is not just limited to this life: "For to me, to live is Christ and to die is gain" (Phil. 1:21). For the cross disciple, all of the Christian life—both now and forever—is predicated on gain.

Finally, although we know the Godhead is self-sufficient and needs nothing, it is also true that God gains from our salvation. When people come to God and find salvation, it glorifies and pleases him. As the book of Hebrews puts it, "without faith it is impossible to please God, because anyone who comes to him must believe that he exists and that he rewards those who earnestly seek him" (Heb. 11:6). Paul also illustrates how we can glorify God by contrasting our earthly, frail, feeble, dust-to-dust bodies with his glorious power at work in and through us: "But we have this treasure in jars of clay to show that this all-surpassing power is from God and not from us" (2 Cor. 4:7).

DEIGN

As the bane of humanity's fall leads us to experience *pain*, and that pain propels us to pursue the *gain* of our salvation, the gain of our salvation enables us to grow taller in the things of God. It is then that we become able to grasp his highest intentions, which far exceed the diminutive thoughts of visionless, nonbelieving people and the dense nature of our fallen humanity. We become empowered to accept, explore, and submit to whatever the Father desires us to do—no matter how costly, grievous, or undesirable it may be. *We learn to deign.*

I know that for some of you this might be a new word, but it is a great one that has great theological implications. The word "deign" possesses several different meanings: to deem beneath oneself, ignore, condescend, accept, submit to, lower oneself, and stoop down to, among others. While "deign" may have a fairly negative connotation today (much like the word "condescend"), originally, to "deign" something was not necessarily viewed as a bad thing. For example, any time God acts toward his creation, he *deigns* to reach down to humanity by stooping down to enter their temporal frame of reference. God is *always* the superior being in any encounter between himself and his creation because he is God, the preeminent One. From the very beginning, God has deigned to interact with human beings and touch their lives in love, even walking with Adam and Eve in the Garden of Eden (Gen. 3:8).

The condescension of God to humanity didn't end with Eden. The entire thrust of Scripture is evidence of the Godhead deigning to enter into history. Consider the formal covenants he made with Abraham (Gen. 12:1–3), Moses (Exod. 19–24), and David (2 Sam. 7:8–29). When God entered into these biblical covenants, he was always the superior person in the agreement. Elsewhere in Scripture, we find God reaching down to individuals to affirm, inform, make promises, and interact with them. God encountered Moses in the burning bush (Exod. 3), Samuel as a voice in the night (1 Sam. 3), and Elijah in the wilderness (1 Kings 19).

So too God deigned to speak to all the Old Testament prophets, such as Jeremiah and Isaiah. In each of these instances, as well as multitudes of others, we find God reaching down to interact with the creation he chose to make.

However, the greatest condescension the Godhead has ever deigned was the incarnation of his Son in human flesh (Heb. 2:14). Jesus completed the Father's work of making a way for human beings to escape the trap the serpent sprang upon them in the garden. His life and death fulfill both the justice and mercy that are part of the nature of the Godhead. His resurrection is proof that humanity will be saved from their sins (1 Cor. 15), become new creatures (2 Cor. 5:17), and join him in eternity in a perfect-purpose relationship that never ends. Thus, the cross is the great dividing point of time: On the one side is hope that our God will rescue us; on the other side is the certainty that he has done so.

Once we have encountered the Lord, grown into cross disciples, and become involved in the process of sanctification, we find ourselves becoming more and more like him. In doing so, we become compelled to *deign* to reach down to others to share the truth about Christ and his riches, to humbly share our wisdom and love as well as witness with those who need to hear it. We reach down to others just as Christ reached down to us. In this manner, *deigning* entails grasping God's bigger reality and the human smaller reality at the same time. The Scripture that makes this truth most clear is Hebrews 12:1b–2 (emphasis added):

> And let us run with perseverance the race marked out for us, fixing our eyes on Jesus, the pioneer and perfecter of faith. For the joy set before him he endured the cross,

scorning its shame, and sat down at the right hand of the throne of God.

As we saw in chapter 1, upon the cross Jesus endured the most horrible, brutal, painful, and agonizing way a person could die. Despite this, joy exploded within him in accomplishing the Father's will in his death, thereby "scorning its shame" (Greek: *kataphronēsas aischunēs*). My favorite translation of this phrase comes from the New Testament for Everyone, which renders this phrase "making light of its shame." I believe this translation gets closest to the meaning and intent of the Savior.

I can't emphasize enough the importance of these two Greek words to my theology and practical life. In Hebrews 12:2, these two words appear after Jesus enduring the cross and before him sitting at the right hand of God, thereby dividing the extremes of the lowest humiliation and the highest exaltation. The word *kataphronēsas* combines the verb *phroneō* ("to think") with the preposition *kata* ("against, down"). It literally means "to think against" or "to think down upon." For Jesus, to *kataphronēsas* shame means that he thought nothing of it, that it never held any power in his mind, that he separated himself from the reality of it, that he knew that it didn't really matter, that he ignored the shame of the event. In "making light" of the disgrace of the cross, Jesus deigned the cost of the cross. He saw the agony of his cross as nothing compared to the ambitions of the Father. The blind rejection of the religious leaders, the injustice of Rome, and the cruel attitude of most of the people certainly hurt Jesus's heart, but none of this affected his mind or thwarted his cross mission!

The cross disciple yearns to imitate Christ, who "scorned the shame" of his cross, rejecting its humiliation. Those who have learned how to deign like Jesus carry their cross like he did. They are enabled to seek a divine love solution that will satisfy and glorify the Lord. If the Father desires it, they

> The cross disciple is therefore one who seeks God's kingdom by reaching down to help others do so as well.

are empowered to do anything at any time and anywhere, no matter how costly, grievous, or undesirable such a deed might be! This includes taking up their cross of self-crucifixion, when necessary, for his will and glory, even when the worldly mind sees such sacrifice as a foolish waste. Cross disciples deign to lower themselves to carry their crosses and to endure horrible pain, knowing the outcome will be rewarded by God. They consent to a lesser action because it confirms and completes the greater action promised by the Father. The cross disciple is therefore one who seeks God's kingdom by reaching down to help others do so as well.

When I reflect on what it means for the cross disciple to deign to reach out to others, I can't help but think back to a few lines from Rich Mullins's song, "The Other Side of the World":

> But the New Jerusalem won't be so easy to build
> There's many bellies to fill and many hearts to free
> Got to set them free
> But I see a people who've learned to walk in faith
> With mercy in their hearts
> And glory on their faces

And I can see the people
And I pray it won't be long
Until Your kingdom comes

The cross disciple is someone who prayerfully seeks his kingdom with a heart full of mercy and a face full of glory and dares to reach down to others to help them become kingdom-seekers as well. Those who are mature in the Lord deign to use their power to separate the good from the bad; they exalt what is excellent and dismiss what is weak. They focus on the truth they have discovered in Christ.

REIGN

Finally, once we become able to reach up to Christ when we *deign* the cross and reach down to others, we discover the power within us to *reign* on earth and steadily overcome all the walls being built around us by our fallen culture and our own sinful natures. *We learn to reign.*

When cross disciples are empowered to deign the agony of the cross and all other struggles as nothing just as Christ did (Heb. 12:2), the ambitions of the Father begin to rule over their lives. As Paul writes:

> For if, by the trespass of the one man, death *reigned* through that one man, how much more will those who receive God's abundant provision of grace and of the gift of righteousness *reign in life* through the one man, Jesus Christ! (Rom. 5:17, emphasis added)

To reign in this life means that we yearn moment by moment for God's presence, yield to his thoughts, and yoke ourselves to his will. Our personal longings become placed under the rule of our sovereign and loving heavenly King. We learn how to put all our issues in Christ, just as the Father has placed us in Christ. To carry our cross continually means we must constantly put ourselves in the presence of the Holy Spirit, where his voice tells us what to think and what to do to complete the will of the Father. This is the master key to living as he intends for us to live.

In doing so, our lives exist for one eternal purpose in the temporary years the Creator has given us: to live out the Lord's mind and mission *in the now*. As a result, we experience the constant reality of the Godhead being with us (Matt. 28:20) as exceedingly more powerful and determinative than all the other realities around us. It is then that we joyfully claim our reign on earth while we wait for his reign. This is what it means to authentically carry one's cross.

Once we reign in this life, we become overcomers (John 16:33). By *believing* and *faith-acting* the Messiah's promises, we can overcome everything that comes at us. This is the Z-Life stage of cross discipleship. The spiritual veterans hear "conquer" as they begin fully comprehending Jesus and his cross. Knowing their Commander intimately, they share his incarnation, cross, and resurrection to a dying world and, in the process, triumph. Cross disciples who learn how to reign are the ultimate conquerors who are equipped to bring glory to the Father in all things and to share his splendor with others. They can touch the world with grace and truth, just as the Messiah did, in order to fulfill the Father's mission (John 1:14). By the energy of daily resurrection, the Z-Life believer steadily gains mastery over their circumstances and becomes better able to control the weaknesses of their sinful nature. The walls of their limitations become vulnerable to God's more perfect plan for their lives. In this manner, the original intention of our Creator Lord is restored (Gen. 1:26–31).

REMAIN

Finally, to *reign* in this life requires that we must *remain* in Christ. The way we are able to maintain our spiritual growth—or recover it after we have experienced a setback—lies in living a life remaining in Christ. Jesus makes this clear in the words he spoke to his disciples the night before his crucifixion:

> "I am the vine; you are the branches. If you *remain* in me and I in you, you will bear much fruit; apart from me you can do nothing. If you do not *remain* in me, you are like a branch that is thrown away and withers; such branches are picked up, thrown into the fire and burned. If you *remain* in me and my words *remain* in you, ask whatever you wish, and it will be done for you. This is to my Father's glory, that you bear much fruit, showing yourselves to be my disciples." (John 15:5–8, emphasis added)

The word "remain" here is the Greek verb *menō*. In the King James Version, *menō* is translated with the English verb "abide." We will discuss in more detail what it means to "abide" in Christ in the next chapter. But for now, the important idea is that unless we "abide" in Jesus, it is impossible for us to triumph as cross disciples and bear any fruit.

If we are to both advance and maintain as much consistency as possible in our cross carrying, we must learn and practice *remaining in Christ*. This is true not just for veteran disciples; *all* believers, no matter what stage they are at in their cross discipleship, must abide in Christ. The A-Life spiritual child needs to try to remain in Christ as much as the Z-Life elder does if he or she wishes to deal with the reality of sin in the world and their lives.

In one of his letters, the apostle John gives us a powerful insight into why it is important for the cross disciple to constantly remain in Christ:

> This is the message we have heard from him and declare to you: God is light; in him there is no darkness at all. If we claim to have fellowship with him and yet walk in the darkness, we lie and do not live out the truth. But if we walk in the light, as he is in the light, we have fellowship with one another, and the blood of Jesus, his Son, purifies us from all sin.
>
> If we claim to be without sin, we deceive ourselves and the truth is not in us. If we confess our sins, he is faithful and just and will forgive us our sins and purify us from all unrighteousness. If we claim we have not sinned, we make him out to be a liar and his word is not in us. (1 John 1:5–10)

Unless we remain in Christ and maintain close fellowship with the Holy Spirit, we will fail to truly live his truth, walk in his light, and understand our sinful condition. Most of all, we must walk in the Spirit and hear his voice. It is only when we continually remain in Christ that we can be in his light, be purified of our unrighteousness, and finally refrain from the self! Only then do we have the confidence and freedom to repeat his life. And this is how you take up your cross daily and follow Jesus!

When someone embarks on becoming a cross-carrying disciple and authentically seeks to repeat the life of Messiah Jesus, he or she will experience five things as he or she grows through the different stages of cross discipleship. First, he or she will experience the *pain* of the tragic bane of the fall. Second, this *pain* will create in them the need to pursue the *gain* of salvation. Third, this *gain* will reveal to them the option to *deign* the cross they bear and reach down to others. Fourth, *deigning* will release the transformative thought enabling them to *reign* in this life while yielding to the Spirit's voice and refraining from the self. Finally, we are only able to *reign* in this life once we have learned to *remain* fully in Christ by abiding in Jesus and bearing fruit.

As we saw in this chapter, authentic growth in Christ will continually bring both pain and gain. But, in putting these two together as the Savior did on the cross by yielding to the Father in obedience and incarnating the resurrection promise, we too will reign in this life like Jesus did. First, however, we must deign the possible cost and agony of the cross as nothing compared to the ambitions and purposes of Christ for us. It is only then that we can authentically play our part in God's drama of redemption and ascend the different stages of cross discipleship.

QUESTIONS FOR REFLECTION

1) What are the five things one experiences when they're on their cross-discipleship journey?

2) How does the experience of *gain* relate to the experience of *pain* in the Christian life? Give a real-life example of how pain can lead to gain for the cross disciple.

3) What does it mean to "deign"? How does Christ serve as an example for us here? How does that relate to reigning in this life?

4) Why is remaining in Christ so important for the cross disciple? What can we learn from John 15 about this?

CHAPTER 6

Three Disciplines of Cross Discipleship

I N THE PREVIOUS TWO CHAPTERS, we explored the three different stages of growth the cross disciple ascends as they transform
from newborn recruits of Christ into adult warriors of the
faith and finally combat veteran leaders who think with the heart
of the cross. From there, we looked at five different experiences
the cross disciple can expect to encounter as they take up their
cross-carrying and cross-hanging missions.

This sixth and final chapter will examine three specific disciplines the cross disciple must adopt in order to flourish in their
mission to take up their cross and follow the Messiah: praise,
prayer, and passion. Now, these certainly aren't the only disciplines
we should practice as cross disciples. Far from it! But as I hope to
show here, praise, prayer, and passion are particularly important
when it comes to playing our role in God's drama of redemption.
They are, as I see it, my triune foundation of following Jesus. I see
him in his constant victories in my life, so I always *praise* him. I
hear his continuous voice, so I am always in *prayer* to him. I have
been called by God to be in spiritual combat for him, so I am full
of *passion* to be victorious for him.

Praise

Praise is our thankful response to what we see God doing in the lives of others and in the world. It is our exclamation confirming that he is our sovereign Lord and all things are moving toward the conclusions desired by him. Perhaps most simply, praise is an uncontrollable joy—you just can't hold it in! Praise means really knowing and living the truth that the Messiah is in charge of everything.

> Perhaps most simply, praise is an uncontrollable joy—you just can't hold it in!

The cross discipline of praise naturally arises when we joyfully perceive the designs and directions for Christ's perfection without complaining about the worldly and fleshly deceits we encounter. It is a marker that our cross-carrying missions are being conducted in good spiritual health. As cross disciples, we must not allow our grief or suffering, setbacks or frustrations, rejections or self-doubt to prevent us from realizing and exalting the higher possibilities and deeper revelations of God's redemptive sacrifice and resurrection promises. In the words of my dear friend, Mickey Bonner (who is now with Christ): "A person's maturity in Christ is always revealed by one's level of praise while undergoing their worst crisis." Amen and amen!

The level of our praise measures everything about us. It illuminates the reality of our love for and trust in Messiah Jesus. It acknowledges that God is bigger than the crisis, the cancer, the conflict, and the crushing you may be experiencing. If you are more focused on the *power of your problems* than on the *power of his promises*, then praise will never dominate your life! The immature of the world are always self-centered and filled with protest; the mature in Christ are always God-centered and filled with praise!

When we truly praise God, we not only offer joyful reverence and pleasure to our Lord but also show others the power that Jesus has over our lives. This is critical! Persistent praise is the most evident and authentic evidence that you can put forth identifying yourself as a cross disciple. Genuine praise demonstrates that you truly perceive his powerful promises and believe that the cross message of Messiah Jesus is the best news that has ever existed. Praise is the great witness that our Savior is more significant and powerful in each of our lives than any human problems or our many flawed desires. It is our shout to the world around us proclaiming that our Savior is Lord and he is in control!

Besides blessing God and demonstrating our faith to the world, true praise also achieves several other things in the life of the cross disciple. It can energize our perception about every pain or perplexity that presses upon us. It can reveal a fresh path guiding our next steps in our cross-carrying missions. It can propel our pursuit of God's presence. Authentic and persistent praise also nurtures our passion to share the excitement of the Messiah's transformative presence in our daily lives with others. Nothing is more effective at changing your heart than adopting an attitude of praise. Finally, continual praise helps keep our lives in orbit around the purposes and plans of the Father. Indeed, there is power in praise that you can't find anywhere else!

One of my favorite memory verses of all time is about the cross discipline of praise. After calling for God's people to rejoice in the Lord, Psalm 149:6 proclaims, "Let the *high praises* of God be in their mouth, and a *two-edged sword* in their hand" (KJV, emphasis added). There are two important things to pay attention to here.

The first one is the use of the phrase "high praise" at the beginning of the verse. The Hebrew word behind this translation is *rommot*, and this is the only place it appears in the entire Old Testament. Not just joy, not just praise, but *high* praise. How about that?

What does high praise mean here? High praise is the utmost level of praise we can reach as human beings. It describes the action of our spirit that most fully captures our purpose as cross disciples, one that floods our mouths with inexpressible hallelujahs of thanksgiving. We reach a state of high praise when we experience the eternality of our sacred calling to proclaim his righteousness as we reign in life. In other words, high praise represents what happens when our minds become completely engulfed in awe as the highest revelations of Christ Jesus become amazingly and compellingly real to our hearts. It is when we can fully yield ourselves to the mind of Christ and demonstrate in word and action the triumph of his crucifixion message in God's redemptive drama.

However, the psalmist doesn't just leave it at that. In addition to the high praise out of our mouths, we are also called to bear a two-edged or double-edged sword in our hands. I have spent a long time reflecting upon what this means. Elsewhere in the Scriptures, we see swords used metaphorically to describe God's Word. In Ephesians 6:17, Paul identifies "the sword of the Spirit" as the Word of God, and Hebrews 4:12 says the Word of God is "sharper than any double-edged sword."

My greatest practical revelation on the matter came to me while watching an interview with a young Australian woman who was struggling with a major drug addiction. Through the help of her Christian friends, she visited a doctor who, after giving her a medical exam, told her, "I can help you deal with the problem of your drug addiction, but you have another problem in your heart, a hole so big that only Jesus could ever fill it." The doctor led her to Christ then and there. At the end of the interview, it was revealed that the woman now ran a home that helped hundreds of young women who were dealing with drug addictions and other problems.

After watching that interview, it hit me that the doctor mentioned in the story was wielding a *double-edged sword*! In the ancient world, a double-edged sword was a dangerous weapon whose blade had two sharp edges, meaning that it could cut from both sides. In the same way, the doctor was truly able to help the young woman because his two-edged sword could hack both the *secular* and the *spiritual* aspects of her life. His life could reach its state of high praise as a cross disciple because he was equipped to deal with both the *earthly matters of our culture* and the *spiritual matters of God's kingdom*! Moreover, the woman also came to live a life of *high praise*! Like the doctor who helped her, she came to possess a double-edged sword of praise by ministering to other women in both secular and spiritual matters.

I believe that Psalm 149:6 tells us that reaching the highest level of praise involves more than simply expressing joy in our Savior. High praise is transformative praise that causes us to change the world around us because the Lord is changing us from within. We can actually feel his power and wisdom come upon us! Such praise only comes about when we are able to handle both the *secular* and *spiritual* aspects of our lives and cut through those two different realities with our two sword "edges." It is only when we have learned how to endure and reign over both our earthly and spiritual realities with our double-edged focus that we can say we are living in high praise. Every Christian should try to live their life in high praise!

First, as cross disciples seeking our highest praise, we must cut through the *secular* aspect of our earthly reality. This means not only being able to cut through the empty deceptions of the world and its fantasies guided by Satan but also being sharp thinkers who have mastered our culture and its secular mindset! The first edge of our sword demands that we have a working grasp of how other people are thinking about our current world, be it economics, politics, education, philosophy, or culture. We must be aware of and comprehend the belief systems active in our secular world. This secular edge of your sword also equips you to be sharp *in the world* and be able to *cut through* the tough moments when it comes to everything from job performance and social involvements to engaging culture and maintaining positive relationships with your peers. We must seek to influence our own little orbit within the secular world according to Christ's mind.

The second "edge" of our sword of high praise must cut deeply into the *spiritual* meanings of God's truth (his standard of reality) and his grace (his initiatives of love) so that we may thrive when it comes to the pardon, power, purpose, plans, and peace he has for our cross-carrying lives. Edge two demands that we know, in depth, the secret things of God through a continuous and growing encounter with the mind, heart, and mission of Messiah Jesus. We must seek to have the Messiah master us and sharpen our minds and hearts in all spiritual matters so that we will be significant for the Father and his sacred agenda! When we are mastered by him, we truly become masters of our lives. Let none of us call Jesus *our Master* when we are living *unmastered* lives in the church!

The *double-edged-sword disciple* brings high praise to God by being effective for Christ in both the *secular* and the *spiritual* arenas of life. When both edges are being used, the cross disciple cannot help but allow the joy and triumph of high praise to come out of their mouth. If true praise is increasing in your life—regardless of your worldly circumstances, current challenges, or personal inner struggles—then you are becoming who you were created (and recreated; see 2 Cor. 5:17–18) to be. You are instinctively and impactfully learning Christ's contentment and sufficiency as you comprehend his peace that surpasses all understanding (Phil. 4:4–7)! Nothing on earth can fill and satisfy the cross disciple's heart more magnificently than to see the blazing and stunning realities of our Lord's life and his message that he wants us for himself! What greater thrill is there than to continue to grasp his supreme significance—his glory and splendor—by playing our part in his drama of redemption and yielding our freedom to his cross control?

May the cross discipline of praise propel us all!

PRAYER

Like praise, prayer is a marker that the cross-carrying duty of the Christian is being taken up in good spiritual health. Authentic prayer is an invitation to speak with and listen to God in conversation. As I have defined it in the past, prayer is "yielding dialogue with him."

While I have many books in my library about the cross discipline of prayer, the most insightful lessons I ever learned on the subject came from J. Sidlow Baxter. Sidlow was my greatest spiritual mentor (some of you might know this). For twenty-five wonderful years in my later life, he was the constant spiritual father I never had. One of the very first lessons Sidlow ever taught me was about prayer.

It still remains one of the most authentic and advanced things I have ever learned about prayer to this day! Isn't that something?

During the first of his many preaching visits to University Baptist Church, Sidlow asked me to pick him up from his hotel at 6:45 a.m. for a morning men's Scripture study. I remember calling his room at 6:30 to make sure that he was awake. When Sid answered the phone, I joked and said, "I hope I didn't wake you up." His answer will be in my mind and heart forever. "Oh, no, dear Harvey, I was simply waiting on you and lingering in prayer!" That fourteen-word sentence *revolutionized* my thinking about prayer. His brief answer not only changed my life at the time, but it has increasingly influenced me every day since.

This idea of "lingering in prayer" was a completely new and dynamic thought for me. *The Merriam-Webster Dictionary* defines the verb "linger" as "to be slow in parting or quitting something." Sid was so delighted and caught up in the reality of prayer—engaging in real dialogue with God and yielding his heart to God's presence—that he hated to leave it and wanted to linger as long as he could, knowing that he was talking to the Father. That must have been what prayer was like for Jesus when he would leave his disciples to pray to his Father alone (Matt. 14:23)!

Lingering is an essential aspect of the cross discipline of prayer. To linger in prayer means never wanting to stop being in dialogue with the Father. To linger in prayer means closely pondering each and every request and subject as you speak with the Father. To linger in prayer means asking the Godhead that every person in your life might come to know more fully the splendor and mystery of seeking, discovering, taking, thinking, carrying, and enduring Jesus's cross as the Holy Spirit's voice leads us! To think that such a profound, natural, and long-lasting lesson about prayer could come from such a simple word.

The importance of lingering wasn't the only lesson about prayer that Sidlow taught me. Throughout his writings (Sidlow wrote thirty books with two of them selling more than a million copies each), he identified four progressive reasons why we pray. First, we pray out of *necessity*—we or someone whom we love may be sick, injured, or suffering and in need of prayer. Second, we pray out of *duty*—to bless a meal, to close a meeting, or as part of some other activity where prayer is a common aspect. Third, we pray in response to our *privilege*—we engage in prayer out of thankfulness for God's many blessings for us, for our families, and for our friends. Fourth, we pray out of *delight*—we come to God solely because we find joy and pleasure in conversing with him. This last type of prayer is the least common of the four. In our free moments, very few of us choose to delight in prayer with the Father as opposed to playing a game, watching TV, or pursuing some other sort of entertainment.

For many years, these four reasons served as my basic framework for understanding prayer. Indeed, all four are true, maturing, and biblical. One day, however, the Holy Spirit once again spoke to me through Sidlow, and I was carried into another one of the great revelations and deep heavenly visions of my life. During the last years of Sidlow's life, Shirley and I would fly to California every February to celebrate his birthday with him. On this particular occasion, he was ninety-six and I was sixty-seven; he had been in the battle of faith for over eighty-five years!

Sidlow and I were sitting in my rental car on the beach at Santa Barbara looking at the Pacific Ocean and talking about the Savior and, particularly, prayer. I casually referred to his four types of prayer when he excitedly announced that the Savior had shown him a fifth type. He paused briefly; I could hardly wait for him to speak. After all, what could be greater than *delight*? Then, looking at the Pacific as though it were a heavenly vision—overcome with evident pleasure and speaking in his beautiful English accent—he said one word with a sense of finality: *absorption*. Once again, my mentor had discovered the right word to talk about prayer!

To become *absorbed* means to fully take in or drink something up, to become captivated and spellbound, to become entirely engrossed and fascinated with something. It means becoming deeply and utterly consumed, like a champion athlete becomes absorbed in their sport. When we partake in this fifth type of prayer, we enter our deepest, most sacred intimacy with Jesus and start living out the Z-Life. We enter a state where *we are truly abiding in him*. A true prayer champion of Christ becomes absorbed in Jesus.

In the previous chapter, I briefly discussed how abiding in the Savior is a central aspect of our experience as cross disciples as we undergo spiritual growth from the A-Life to the Z-Life. As Jesus so insightfully says in the Gospel of John, "I am the vine; you are the branches. If you remain [Greek: *menō*] in me and I in you, you will bear much fruit; apart from me you can do nothing" (John 15:5). Unless we remain in Christ, we can never experience the triumph of taking up our cross and following him. We must abide in our Lord each and every moment so that we may realize he truly is our all in all!

It is in those moments where we as cross disciples authentically become absorbed in prayer that we are truly able to experience abiding in our Savior. Here, I think of John 17, a passage that Sidlow often referred to when speaking about this type of prayer.

While praying to the Father on behalf of all who believe in him, Jesus asked God, "that all of them may be one, Father, just as you are in me and I am in you. May they also be in us so that the world may believe that you have sent me. I have given them the glory that you gave me, that they may be one as we are one—I in them and you in me" (John 17:21–23a). That we might become one with God and his Son—that we might increasingly become absorbed in Christ and share in his splendor in everything we say and do—should be the deepest desire and passion of our hearts! And it is through the cross discipline of prayer that we can pursue that desire of absorption with him.

It doesn't matter what's going on in your life right now, how busy or stressed or distracted you might be. It doesn't matter how great things might be or how impossible things might seem. It doesn't matter how empty your current prayer life may be or whether you feel like a prayer novice. (Good night, I'm still a novice in the ways of prayer myself!) As Christians, prayer is our ultimate resource because it invites God to abide in us and through us, empowering us to play our parts in his drama of redemption and ascend through the stages of cross discipleship.

As I've heard it said, the point isn't about mastering prayer but rather allowing God *to master us through prayer*! I urge you to strive continually to master those five steps of prayer, for to learn to pray rightly moves everything in your life closer to the Lord's right direction.

Passion

The final cross discipline I would like to talk about here is passion. It was 1954 when I first remember paying close attention to John 2:17. I still remember how I was gripped by this fresh and explosive thought impressed upon me by the Holy Spirit, and the verse's precept, sentiment, and battle cry has burned in my heart ever since! According to John, after the disciples watched Jesus drive out the sacrificial animals and money changers from the courts of the Jerusalem Temple, they remembered the words from a psalm of David: "Zeal for your house will consume me" (Ps. 69:9).

I could spend the rest of this chapter discussing why David originally said those words, why the disciples saw Jesus as the prophetic fulfillment of this psalm, and all the many nuances of the Hebrew and Greek words for "zeal" and "consume" here. For our present purposes, however, I would like to focus specifically on what this verse can teach us about the discipline of passion.

To start, like Jesus in his Father's temple, the cross disciple must be *consumed* by their zeal—their passion—for the purposes and desires of our Messiah. To be consumed is to have your life totally used up, to have your every thought, hope, and dream be focused upon one central thing. When Jesus was in the temple, he was filled with fiery passion because his Father's house was being dirtied by the sale of animals by so-called worshipers who were greedily seeking to make money. Jesus was *consumed with zeal* because the worship of his Father was being cheapened.

To become consumed with the same passion that Jesus had in the temple can only happen if your supreme ambition and agenda are to follow the Master daily! The cross disciple who is zealously consumed by the purposes and desires of the Messiah can't devour enough of the Savior's heart, know enough of the Savior's mind, feel enough of the Savior's love, or accomplish enough of the Savior's will. Our greatest and most intense interest on earth should always be *to know Christ and to make him known*!

Next, the word "zeal" can be translated many other ways: passion, devotion, diligence, drive, eagerness, fervor, and intensity, among other synonyms. Our English word "zeal" is derived from the Greek word *zēlos* used in John 2:17, which is the same word used by Paul in 2 Corinthians 7:7 to describe the Corinthians' fervent, loving concern for him.

Zeal or passion does not mean perfection. Once, when I was at a luncheon with my friend Frank Broyles—the legendary Arkansas Razorback football coach and athletic director—someone posed the question: "What is the most essential quality of a great athlete?" After several of us floated different answers, Frank finally spoke up, giving a brief but pointed response: "No one will ever be the top athlete—a champion—unless he or she exhibits a *total passion to do their best*." Being consumed with passion will not make us perfect, but it will push us to be the *best possible disciples* we can be until our death. It will compel us to trust the Holy Spirit with every inch of ourselves and leave the results in God's hands. This should be the motto of every cross disciple!

When the cross disciple is consumed by their zealous passion for Messiah Jesus and yearns to advance his lordship over their life, they will find that their

> Being consumed with passion will not make us perfect, but it will push us to be the *best possible disciples* we can be until our death.

thoughts and dreams begin to change. They will find themselves constantly dreaming about and wanting to know more about Jesus, to live more authentically for him, and to become ever more unified with him in his cross and resurrection. If we as cross disciples ever find that this isn't the case, then we need to deepen our daily time with him, allow our hearts to become more broken, and reexamine our comprehension of his cross.

Our dreams tell us everything about what we truly desire and hope for as well as reflect how we're dealing with our past experiences, what our present mindset is, and what we hold to be our future purpose. So, I say to you as well as to myself: Are our current dreams zealously consumed with the purposes and will of Jesus? Can we feel all our dreams being changed to increasingly please him?

This question reminds me of one of my favorite dramatic musicals. In a scene from *Fiddler on the Roof*, Tevye's daughter Chava tells him about the gentile boy she is determined to marry. But Tevye, who is adamant about clinging to the old, familiar ways, is against this marriage since the boy is not Jewish. In response, Chava pleads with Tevye, "But Papa, he has changed the shape of all my dreams!" This should be our response as well to the love and call of Messiah Jesus to play our small parts in his drama of redemption. When his purpose, joy, and passion truly consume us, our hopes and dreams are reshaped to match his concerns, commands, and cross. Our answer then, as cross disciples, should always be to fervently exclaim, "He has changed and is changing the shape of all my dreams!"

In my own life, I have felt my thoughts and dreams become transformed by an urgency and hunger to be an agent, spokesman, teacher, friend, example, and ambassador of his cross who, through the power of the Holy Spirit, seeks to connect as many people as possible to the grace and truth of our Lord Jesus. When I reflect theologically upon my personal experience of this consuming passion for my cross-carrying mission, three particular passages of Scripture stand out to me.

First, I think of the words of Jeremiah when, regarding God calling him to be a prophet, he declared, "His word is in my heart like a fire, a fire shut up in my bones, and I am weary of holding it in. Indeed, I cannot!" (Jer. 20:9b). Like Jeremiah, when God's love and consuming zeal burns within us, we deeply *yearn* to share the message of his life-giving cross with others, so much so that our passion to exalt Lord Jesus and to help others radically conforms our attitudes and actions to be like the Savior's. It is this same burning zeal that compelled Messiah Jesus to leave the perfection of heaven and deign to reach down to his Father's creation of helpless, harassed, and hopeless people on earth in order to save them (Luke 19:10)! But like Jeremiah, we must strive not to allow our old sinful self to hold back our zeal for his perfect cross-carrying mission.

Second, following my retirement from University Baptist Church, one Gospel saying that has constantly been on my mind is Jesus's instruction to Martha in Luke 10. Upon arriving at the house of Martha and her sister Mary, Jesus began teaching. As Jesus taught, Martha continued to make preparations for her guests while Mary sat at Jesus's feet listening to his words. Feeling frustrated, Martha approached Jesus and said, "Lord, don't you care that my sister has left me to do the work by myself? Tell her to help me!" (Luke 10:40b). Good night, it's hard to believe she made such an audacious misstatement, isn't it? It is then that Jesus said these words:

"Martha, Martha," the Lord answered, "you are worried and upset about many things, but few things are needed—or indeed only one. Mary has chosen what is better, and it will not be taken away from her." (Luke 10:41–42)

The one necessary thing that Jesus references here is Mary's zealous desire to yearn for him, yield to him, and become yoked with him. Just like Mary, we must also yearn to sit at the feet of our Master and allow our passion to understand his cross to consume us and shape our attitudes and actions. But we must first be able to disregard the "many things" that are unnecessary in our lives.

Unlike Martha, we must not let the "preparations" of daily life—the things that won't last forever—distract us from the eternal things that really matter! As authentic cross disciples, we must be mindful, wise, secure, and calm like Mary whenever we encounter circumstances and challenges that might worry us or distract us from sitting at the feet of the Master. In the words of 2 Peter 1:3, we must remember that God's divine power is "everything we need for a godly life through our knowledge of him who called us by his own glory and goodness."

Being mindful like Mary about acting out our passion to hear our Savior is not easy. Through more than seventy years of struggling and striving to be a cross disciple of Jesus, I have become convinced that *mindlessness about the meaning of our daily cross* is one of our greatest oversights, flaws, and vulnerabilities as Christians! Like Martha, we steadily become distracted by or worried about all of our issues and problems. But when we do that, we also become distracted from his key truth! God cannot transform our dreams, hearts, or actions with maximum spiritual impact until we can set aside all our distractions, seek out the mind of Christ, and allow it to consume us. Our only true hope for overcoming the challenges and calamities of this world is to focus upon his cross and divine power every moment of our lives. We must exchange our minds for his and quit thinking with our fallen and flawed hearts that become distracted with unnecessary worries. In the words of Jesus, we must always "seek first [the Father's] kingdom" in all aspects of our daily lives (Matt. 6:33).

Third, when I reflect on the consuming passion for the Savior that we, as cross disciples, must embrace, I cannot help but think of Paul's words in 2 Timothy:

> For I am already being poured out like a drink offering, and the time for my departure is near. I have fought the good fight, I have finished the race, I have kept the faith. Now there is in store for me the crown of righteousness, which the Lord, the righteous Judge, will award to me on that day—and not only to me, but also to all who have longed for his appearing. (2 Tim. 4:6–8)

Entering the ninth decade of my life on this earth—what I like to call my "sunset decade" or "awakening dawn" period of life—I have recently learned much about the cross discipline of passion. I feel as if Paul's words have become my own as I have sought to comprehend how to fight the good fight and pour out my life for Christ and others as the time of my own departure is coming closer. I definitely want to fulfill the ministry path that I still see set before me by the Master! I have tried to let every moment in my life be guided by my passion for him as I run the last leg of this great race with patience and endurance, always fixing my eyes on Jesus.

What I truly find amazing is that in this sunset period, I feel that I have discovered the most thrilling and highest dimension of cross discipleship I've encountered in my life. As I have come ever closer to "finishing the race," the Lord has marked out for me, I have experienced an increased sense of urgency and zeal for embracing and enduring my cross. I have never been more excited, content, expectant, grateful, humbled, eager, and confident about the Lord Jesus loving me, forgiving me, and using me in his purposes of grace and truth, even though I truly sense that I am one of his most unworthy, undependable, unknowing, and unprofitable servants! My deepest dream is to tell *everyone* about his splendorous patience, pardon, promises, power, and presence that he has made so real to me in my attempt at living the cross-carrying life! Even so, I still deeply regret those times I didn't fix my eyes on Jesus and the moments I failed to yield to the Holy Spirit's voice.

As Paul writes in Philippians, even though the Lord Jesus was truly God, he nevertheless humbly made himself nothing, deigning to reach down to humanity, in order to fulfill the cross mission his Father gave him (Phil. 2:5–11)! At last, in this sunset period of my life, I can say that I am stunningly, brokenly, thrillingly, and finally able to recognize that same supreme ambition in myself! I yearn as never before to be *nothing to myself* so I might expectantly become *the Father's someone* to increasingly fulfill all of his desires! There remains in my heart a fire that I cannot restrain; a need to sit before my Master's feet that I cannot quench! I earnestly want to tell everyone I can about the cross of our Messiah.

I know my time on earth is running out, but I still yearn for the months ahead—be they one or one hundred—so that I can be the most zealous cross disciple that I can possibly be. I have no fear, only a relaxed urgency to fully please our dear Savior while I can! Blessed indeed are all those who are zealously on that journey of daily cross revelation, cross response, and cross resurrection. May we all have such passion to be consumed by our Savior's call to cross discipleship!

GENERAL CURTIS LEMAY, THE FORMER United States Air Force chief of staff, once addressed a group of new officers with the following words: "To you new, young generals I would say this: If you are in command, then take command!" I can think of few truer statements when it comes to our mission as cross disciples. The Lord has put *you* in charge of *you*! Your decisions and your actions are *your* creation responsibility!

Throughout this book, I have examined how Christ's cross and sacrifice not only represent the greatest scene in God's drama of redemption, reconciliation, and salvation, but also model for us how we, as his followers, must obey the words of Luke 9:23 and take up our own crosses and follow him! Fewer things are more important to that mission than being propelled by *praise*, absorbed by *prayer*, and consumed by *passion* for his desires and purposes. When we joyfully praise our Savior in both word and deed, authentically abide in the Holy Spirit through prayer, and allow our hopes and dreams to become zealously consumed by his call, we will find ourselves incarnating ever more closely the cross-carrying and cross-hanging life of our Lord Jesus. But, it is *our* duty and responsibility to practice these cross disciplines in our daily lives and allow them to transform who we are into who we were created to be by the Father.

Questions for Reflection

1) Define what "praise" is. How does this differ from "high praise"? What does it mean to wield high praise like a "double-edged sword"?

2) Name the five different reasons why we pray as cross disciples. Give an example of each type of prayer and explain why that particular form is important for the cross-carrying life.

3) What does it mean to "linger" in prayer? How does the idea of lingering change how you view your own prayer life?

4) What does it mean to be "consumed by passion" as a cross disciple? What are some practical ways you could exercise that passion in your daily life?

CONCLUSION

What Kind of Disciple Will You Be?

As I mentioned in the introduction to this book, the only time Jesus explicitly mentions the cross in the New Testament Gospels is when he commands his disciples to take up their cross and follow him. Five different times in the New Testament, Jesus makes it clear that being his disciple requires carrying a cross (Matt. 10:38, 16:24; Mark 8:34; Luke 9:23, 14:27). I have found two of these verses especially powerful:

> "And whoever does not carry their cross and follow me cannot be my disciple." (Luke 14:27)

> "Whoever does not take their cross and follow me is not worthy of me." (Matt. 10:38)

The total meaning of these two verses is that you must do more than simply seek to know the cross Jesus calls you to carry. *You must actually take it up.* This isn't just an optional feature of one's Christian faith, for as Jesus himself says, this is the essential part of our very identity as his worthy followers. Cross carrying is the primary task of being his disciple—without it, we aren't really his disciples at all!

Throughout the previous chapters, I have tried to demonstrate what it looks like to seek out, discover, and hang upon the cross that Jesus calls us each to carry. This must be our greatest passion—our endgame in life! In the words of Hebrews 12:1–2, we have each been called to run in perseverance a great race in life. And while each of us may have a different race to run, a different target to hit, or a different type of cross to carry, at the end of the day, this is what it means to be a Christian, and nothing less! Whatever the cost, we must be willing to pay it!

All that being said, by no means is this cross-carrying mission solely a dark and horrible battle. While carrying your cross may be the most difficult trial you'll ever encounter, I can promise you that it is also the most thrilling and joy-filled journey you will ever take! On this subject, I love the words of the apostle Paul:

> However, I consider my life worth nothing to me; my only aim is to *finish* the race and complete the task the Lord Jesus has given me—the task of *testifying to the good news of God's grace.* (Acts 20:24, emphasis added)

Paul nails it for each of us here. There are three aspects of this verse that I find especially meaningful. First, each of our cross-carrying missions are anchored in the gospel—the *good news of God's grace.* In Old English, the word "gospel" literally means "good news." However, I think "good news" is a massive understatement. It is *great* news—the *greatest* good news that has ever come to this earth!

Second, according to Paul, the cross-carrying races we have been commanded to run call for us to *testify* about Jesus's love and sacrifice to save all humanity. The Greek word Paul uses here (*diamarturasthai*) that is translated as the verb "testify," comes from the Greek noun *martys*, the same word from which we get "martyr." When Paul speaks of "testifying to the good news," he is saying that our speech about Jesus should be earnest, joyous, and convincing, even though it may lead us down a road of tremendous sacrifice and suffering. But, for Paul, the good news of this message far outweighs the potential sacrifice!

Finally, Paul states that life is worth nothing to him unless he is able to *finish* the race he has been called to run. The Greek verb Paul employs here (*teleiōsai*) is the *exact same verb* that Jesus pronounced from the cross when he gave up his spirit (John 19:30). Like Jesus, Paul had his own cross to bear to completion—and so do we! We, like Jesus and Paul, must be willing to deny ourselves and carry our crosses until the very end of the missions assigned to us when we, too, may rejoice in pronouncing *it is finished*.

During one of my first seasons serving as the chaplain of the Arkansas Razorback football team, I remember spending an afternoon at a linebacker practice. I watched as the coach ran his players through a series of intense tackling drills. As we walked off the field at the end of practice, I could see all the athletes were completely exhausted. They were drenched in sweat, and some were even visibly bruised and bleeding. In the midst of the silence, I offered the coach a nugget of my novice coaching "wisdom" as we walked: "Well, Coach, looks like you have some great players here." After more than fifty years, I can still hear his reply. "I don't know yet, Reverend," he said. "I still have to figure out which ones just want to be football players and which ones really want to play football!" In that brief moment, he summarized what I see as being the greatest weakness in the church today—too many of us are content simply being called Christians, but only a few of us are truly determined to follow Christ!

Every person who calls himself or herself a Christian should ask themselves the same question: Am I content simply being labeled a Christian and wearing my "church uniform"? Or, are my attitudes and actions truly centered on seeking, carrying, and suffering upon the sacrificial cross Christ calls me to bear? In other words, am I content merely being a *casual disciple* sitting on the sidelines, or am I truly willing to embrace with passion the costly sacrifice that it takes to be an authentic, active, and advancing *cross disciple*?

Looking back upon my life, during my younger years I was definitely a casual and senseless disciple at best! Sure, I started attending church when I was eleven, and over time I began to know *about* Jesus. I was even baptized, although I had no idea what that really meant. I might have labeled myself a Christian as a young teenager, but I didn't know Jesus personally. It wasn't until my senior year of high school that I became a true *cross disciple* and experienced God's presence and power in a way I had never dreamed possible. I can still remember what I said when I made that first prayer of repentance, sorrow, need, and faith: "Lord Jesus, I don't understand all this life and faith business, but I know I really need to be more than I am. Please forgive me for all the wrong things I have done and thought. I ask you to please come into my life and be my Savior and Lord and make me what you created me to be! Thank you for saving me and giving me a new life!"

As I hope to have shown in this book, through the *agonizing and redemptive death of Jesus our Messiah*, you and I have all been chosen and called to be recreated as his cross disciples. That same cross that brought salvation and reconciliation for our broken world also models how we should respond to the Savior's great and mysterious act of sacrificial love in the cosmic *drama of redemption*. The way Jesus obeyed God's will, drank from his cup, and fulfilled his duty by hanging upon the cross teaches us how to adapt to our own cross missions that we have been called to and *endure the suffering* that comes with that duty. So too the *seven final sayings* of Jesus as he was being crucified reveal how we, as cross disciples, must always be forgiving, ministering, remembering, seeking, suffering, finishing, and trusting as we bring Jesus to others. Of course, none of us will ever do this perfectly. As we saw, cross discipleship is a *life-long process of growth* as we gradually ascend from being spiritual newborns focusing on the ABCs of Christianity to becoming adult warriors engaged in the spiritual battle of the MNOPs of our faith and then, finally, veteran fathers and mothers who have started to master the XYZs of our cross-disciple lives. Nor will this be easy. Every cross disciple will have to experience the *pains* of our fallen world before reaching the *gains* of the Savior's salvation. And only once the cross disciple is able to reach down to others and *deign* the suffering of their cross mission will they truly be able to *reign* over their lives, as long as they *remain* in the Godhead. Such a self-sacrificial process requires a life propelled by *praise*, a heart absorbed in *prayer*, and a mind consumed with *passion* for the Savior's purposes in order to be successful in the Father's eyes.

Cross discipleship isn't a walk in the park—it's spiritual warfare, a battle that covers every single moment of your life. And it will be that way until Jesus returns. All of us will encounter more than our fair share of struggles and mistakes as we attempt to understand his cross and ours. Good night, I'll be the first to admit that I don't know all the answers here. I'm just one little struggler like everyone else! At the end of the day, you and I will never be able to fully understand (much less explain) the cross of Jesus Christ and the mysterious love of our Messiah any more than a two-year-old could have any possible idea what it meant for their mother to become pregnant and suffer incredible pain to give birth to them. Yet, while a toddler may not be able to comprehend the miracle of birth or their mother's sacrifice, they do understand that their mother loves them and that their future is safe with her. *All their moments are dedicated to their mothers.* You and I are the same way; our little human brains will *never* fully be able to grasp the wonderful depth and magnificence of what Christ did for us on the cross. But I'll tell you this: I know that Christ loves me and I have an eternal future with him. And frankly, my dear friends, I don't need anything else—and neither do you! To paraphrase the words of the gospel singer George Beverly Shea, while I may not know much about Jesus and his cross, what little I know has changed my life!

> I know that Christ loves me and I have an eternal future with him. And frankly, my dear friends, I don't need anything else—and neither do you!

As I said in the introduction, my goal in this book was to explore what Jesus truly meant when he commanded his disciples to take up their crosses and follow him. I must confess that even now as I write this conclusion, I still feel that I have only scratched the surface of this topic—despite all my theological research and prayerful reflection. However, one thing I do know is that far too often, our response in our hearts to Jesus's command is "I'll take it up tomorrow," or "I'll bear my cross next week," or "I'll follow him after I get some things straightened out." However, if you really want to take up your cross and follow him, you just need to do it *right now*! No other time will do. Do not hold out or delay on his calling any longer!

Acknowledgments

Special Thanks

To my wife, Shirley, my daughter, Karen, and my son-in-law, Mark, who have supported and loved me as we have navigated seeing this book come to fruition. In memory of my precious son, Kevin, who loved his family and whose heart was toward the Lord.

To my grandchildren, Ashley (Kurt), Alyssa (Charlie), Will (Cris), Andrea (Brian), Hayden, and Landon, who have always been my joy and encouragement!

To my precious nine great-grandchildren, Evy Kate, Liam, Lynley, Lukie, Ruby, Mabry, Haddon, Lois, and Hallie Kay. You bring delight and help me see the Father clearly!

To my Ventures for Christ board, for their continuous wisdom and support as we seek to make the Lord Jesus known: Scott Bull, Ken Stuckey, Jim Benton, David Williams, Gus Rusher, Bill Bradley, Jim Barnes, Mark Marquess, Howard Hamilton, Bobby New, West Doss, Richard Green, Jim Lindsey, and Lyndy Lindsey.

To Scott Bull (chairman, Ventures) and Ken Stuckey (associate chairman, Ventures), who kept pushing for this book to happen, and giving their love and wisdom along the way.

To Jim Benton, who made this book financially possible and whom I have had the privilege of knowing since his college days.

To Ruth Ann Stites, for her research and publication work, and Rita Dunkelberger, for her organizational and pastoral support work, and to the rest of my excellent Ventures staff for your support in so many ways.

To James Barnett, Tom Dean, and Blake Jurgens, for your expertise, brilliance, and patience in the editing and writing process!

To Bernie Holstein, widow of Verd Holstein, who led me to Christ back in 1950, how can gratitude ever be adequately expressed?

To all who have touched my life and the Lord Jesus has used to teach me, shape me, humble me, and change me: thank you for the blessing and privilege of knowing you!

To our precious Lord Jesus, whose sandals I am definitely unworthy to tie, but whose ultimate example of cross-bearing has transformed my life!

Ventures for Christ

Although I left my position with University Baptist Church after thirty-nine years of pastoral ministry, that was by no means the end of my cross mission! For the past two decades, I have continued to serve Christ and minister to those living here in Arkansas as well as around the world through Ventures for Christ.

Ventures was started by Jim Lindsey and myself in the spring of 1972 as a parachurch organization to raise money and support for various ministries and evangelism opportunities across Arkansas. As the chaplain for the Razorbacks, I had many calls and requests for athletes to share their Christian testimonies to youth organizations. With the encouragement and help of Jim Lindsey and Frank Broyles (Arkansas's head football coach at the time), Ventures raised funds to cover the travel and expenses needed for these athletes to share with hundreds of young people. Bill Burnett, one of Arkansas's greatest football players, caught the vision for this opportunity, knowing it would have a huge impact across the state. With Ventures's support, Bill became the first state director for Fellowship of Christian Athletes. Other states would soon follow Arkansas's lead in naming directors for this organization.

Ventures formed a board of directors to give oversight and direction to accomplish the purpose of sharing Christ and encouraging people in their faith. I became president of Ventures and had the desire to continue to love and reach out to students and others I had known throughout my years of ministry. After retiring from full-time ministry in 2004, Ventures has served as a way to continue the ministry work I started at University Baptist Church, as well as increasingly impact people searching for clarity, empowerment, and intimacy with our living and reigning Lord, both here in Fayetteville and across the globe. Ventures is blessed to give to many disciplers, missionaries, and special mission emphases all over the world in our desire to have an international impact for the Lord Jesus.

The main reason that prompted me to become fully involved with Ventures was God's call for me to enter into a new stage of ministry life—my so-called sunset decade! I am deeply grateful to the Savior for my many years as a senior pastor, air force chaplain, regional television figure, newspaper columnist, and adjunct Bible professor—not to mention my three decades as a chaplain for college athletes as the "Razorback Rabbi" at the University of Arkansas! But praise God, now that those busy years are over, God has gifted me a new, fruitful period of life, one where I can take the time to reflect more deeply upon his Word and share more effectively the motivating and compelling insights that have marked my little life through his generous grace.

One of the major ways I have sought to fulfill my urgent cross duty with Ventures for Christ in these last years of life has been to concentrate on writing. I want to use this medium to bring God's redeeming presence to thousands. Through the financial and prayer investments of so many individuals, we have been able to produce dozens of brochures, booklets, and other resources that have exposed people to the cross life and brought them into cross discipleship. In addition, we have been able to produce a number of videos reflecting on a range of theological topics including Trinitarian thinking (you, your issue, and God), living an impactful life in light of Christ's cross, and what it truly means to experience Christ now and in our later years.

Our only goal at Ventures has always been to make our own lives worth something for Jesus's sake and to lead others to do the same. We passionately and urgently believe this is our kingdom call as cross disciples! Ever since we started Ventures, we have sought fresh ways to help other hungry disciples exchange their worldly minds for the mind of Christ concerning all issues. Our most earnest desire is to help enable the spiritually hungry from all walks of life to overcome the deception, drift, dullness, and defeat of this world by grasping the clear, immediate, and liberating teachings of the life of Christ and the cross.

Ventures has been a wonderful tool that God has given me to express my joy and love for the Messiah to the world. I am truly grateful for what the Lord has done through our various ministry initiatives, and I am excited to see what he will continue to do through this ministry in the months (and years!) to come. All of us here at Ventures for Christ warmly invite you to visit our website (venturesforchrist.com) and join us on the Christ-life journey as we seek out his grace, his truth, his promises, and his cross. On our website, you'll find dozens of articles, sermons, and videos as well as a link to partner financially in our mission to know Christ and make him known!

Notes

All University Baptist sermons referenced here can be found on the Ventures for Christ YouTube channel at https://www.youtube.com/@venturesforchrist7559.

All messages from the Dr. H. D. McCarty YouTube channel referenced here can be found at https://www.youtube.com/@dr.h.d.mccarty4348/featured.

Introduction

The word "cross" (*stauros* in Greek) appears in Matthew 10:38, Matthew 16:24, Mark 8:34, Luke 9:23, and Luke 14:23 in the New Testament Gospels, although one might read the notion of the cross into John 6:56: "Whoever eats my flesh and drinks my blood remains in me, and I in them." In some cases, the cross saying of Jesus includes the statement: "Whoever does not take their cross and follow me is not worthy of me" (Matt. 10:38).

The story of the second lieutenant originally appeared in my sermon, "The Cross: Our Magnificent Obsession" preached at University Baptist Church.

Chapter 1: The Crucifixion of Jesus and the Drama of Redemption

I could name countless books and articles from the past several decades that have influenced my understanding of Jesus's crucifixion and its historical context. Here, I will restrict myself to the main sources that guided the research for this chapter.

Regarding the entire crucifixion narrative in Scripture and its historical context, see Craig Evans and N. T. Wright, *Jesus, the Final Days: What Really Happened* (Louisville: Westminster John Knox, 2009); David Wallace Chapman and Eckhard J. Schnabel, *The Trial and Crucifixion of Jesus: Texts and Commentary*, 2nd ed. (Peabody, MA: Hendrickson, 2019); Raymond E. Brown, *The Death of the Messiah*, 2 vols. (Garden City, NY: Doubleday, 1994). For an accessible popular essay on the subject, see theologian Michael F. Bird, "The Horror of Crucifixion," Word from the Bird (blog), March 9, 2022, https://michaelfbird.substack.com/p/the-horror-of-crucifixion.

Regarding Jesus's arrest and trial, see R. P. Booth, "We Have a Law . . .": The Trials of Jesus of Nazareth," *Denning Law Journal* 6.1 (1991): 1–21.

Regarding crucifixion in the ancient world, see Gunnar Samuelsson, *Crucifixion in Antiquity: An Inquiry into the Background and Significance of the New Testament Terminology of Crucifixion*, 2nd ed. (Tübingen: Mohr Siebeck, 2013); John Granger Cook, *Crucifixion in the Mediterranean World*, 2nd ed. (Tübingen: Mohr Siebeck, 2019).

For Herodotus's report of Darius the Great's use of crucifixion, see *Histories* 3.159.1; 7.194.1–3. Alexander the Great's crucifixion of the men of Tyre is recounted by the first-century BC Greek historian Diodorus Siculus in his *Library of History* 17.46.4. For

Josephus's discussion of Alexander Jannaeus's use of crucifixion, see his *Antiquities* 13.380.

Appian's account of the Roman crucifixion of the participants of Spartacus's slave rebellion can be found in his *Roman History* 1.120. For Josephus's report of the Roman crucifixion of Jewish rebels in AD 70, see his *Jewish War* 5.449–451.

Ancient authors who report Roman crucifixion of women and even children include Tacitus, *Annals* 14.42–45; Josephus, *Jewish War* 2.306–308. Peter's method of crucifixion is mentioned by, among others, the early Christian theologian Tertullian in his *Antidote for the Scorpion's Sting* 15. Among others mentioning Paul's beheading, see the famous ancient church historian Eusebius, *Church History* 2.25.

For Cicero's firsthand account of crucifixion and its brutality, see his *Against Verres* 5.168–170. Among other Roman writers describing the beating of crucifixion victims, see Cicero, *Against Verres* 2.14; Dionysius of Halicarnassus, *Roman Antiquities* 5.51.3; Josephus, *Jewish War* 6.304. Seneca's description of torture instruments comes from his *Consolation to Marcia* 20.3.

Ancient authors mentioning the patibulum (horizontal crossbeam) and stipes (vertical beam) as well as the carrying of the crossbeam and hanging of crucifixion victims include Plautus, *Carbonaria* 2; Dionysus of Halicarnassus, *Roman Antiquities* 7.69.1–2.

For more on the archeological discovery of the ancient Jewish crucifixion victim Yehohanan, see the Biblical Archaeological Society, "A Tomb in Jerusalem Reveals the History of Crucifixion and Roman Crucifixion Methods," Bible History Daily (blog), August 16, 2022, https://www.biblicalarchaeology.org/daily/

biblical-topics/crucifixion/a-tomb-in-jerusalem-reveals-the-history-of-crucifixion-and-roman-crucifixion-methods/.

Concerning the use of a titulus (placard) describing the crime of the crucifixion victim, see ancient historian Cassius Dio, *Roman History* 54.3.7.

Regarding the medical and physiological aspects of crucifixion, see F. P. Retief and L. Cilliers, "The History and Pathology of Crucifixion," *South African Medical Journal* 93 (2003): 938–41; F. P. Retief and L. Cilliers, "Christ's Crucifixion as a Medico-Historical Event," *Acta Theologica* 26.2 (2006): 294–310.

Ancient authors describing the burial (or lack thereof) of crucifixion victims include Cicero, *Against Verres* 2.45; Philo, *Against Flaccus* 83–85.

Chapter 2: Jesus's Last Words from the Cross
Portions of this chapter have appeared in different forms in various sermons and writings I have produced over the years. See especially the University Baptist Church sermon "Learning How to Hang in There" on the Ventures for Christ YouTube channel as well as "7 Scriptures from the Cross" on the Dr. H. D. McCarty YouTube channel.

Chapter 3: Suffering and Cross Discipleship
Portions of this chapter have appeared in various forms in some of my sermons. Most notably, see the University Baptist sermons "Learning How to Hang in There," "Enduring the Contest of Life," and "The Wondrous Necessity of Suffering" on the Ventures for Christ YouTube channel. Portions have also been taken from my

message "Don't Be Dumb about Your Suffering" on the Dr. H. D. McCarty YouTube channel.

Chapter 4: The Stages of Cross Discipleship
The concept of the U-A-O-Z Life has been discussed in several other formats through my ministry at Ventures for Christ. Regarding 1 John 2 as the biblical basis for the U-A-O-Z Life model, see my message "Three Stages of Growth (1 John 2:12)" on the Dr. H. D. McCarty YouTube channel.

Chapter 5: Experiencing Cross Discipleship
Portions of this chapter were derived from my "Three Stages of Growth (1 John 2:12)" message on the Dr. H. D. McCarty YouTube channel as well as my University Baptist Church sermon "The Wondrous Necessity of Suffering" on the Ventures for Christ YouTube channel.

Chapter 6: Three Disciplines of Cross Discipleship
This chapter draws from several of my University Baptist Church sermons found on the Ventures for Christ YouTube channel, including "A Person of Praise," "The Refreshing Power of Praise," and "Prayer: Your Ultimate Resource."

The notion of "high praise" in Psalm 149 is dealt with in more detail in my messages "Finding High Praise (Ps. 149:6)" and "High Praises and the Double-Edged Sword" on the Dr. H. D. McCarty YouTube channel.

www.ingramcontent.com/pod-product-compliance
Lightning Source LLC
Chambersburg PA
CBHW020247130626
46549CB00005B/2103